BIGFOOT...

IT'S COMPLICATED

A CONGRESSMAN AND FORMER INTELLIGENCE OFFICER EXPLORES
THE POLITICS OF TRUE BELIEVERS: BIGFOOT AND OTHERWISE

DENVER RIGGLEMAN

outskirts
press

Bigfoot...It's Complicated
A Congressman and former Intelligence Officer explores the politics of true believers: Bigfoot and otherwise
All Rights Reserved.
Copyright © 2020 Denver Riggleman
v9.0

Outskirts Press, Inc.
http://www.outskirtspress.com

ISBN: 978-1-4787-5125-0

Library of Congress Control Number: 2018906565

Cover photo by Abigail Riggleman

Outskirts Press and the "OP" logo are trademarks belonging to Outskirts Press, Inc.

PRINTED IN THE UNITED STATES OF AMERICA

TABLE OF CONTENTS

PROLOGUE

The secret thoughts of any man run over all things, holy, profane, clean, obscene, grave, and light, without shame or blame.

-Thomas Hobbes

Is Bigfoot's penis proportionate? I mean, how big was it?

- My Wife

Who's the guy in the monkey suit?

- Michigan State Trooper

When I told my wife that I was going to write a nonfiction book about Bigfoot and Bigfoot Believers, she thought I was nuts. Bigfoot, although seen on Discovery Channel, the Travel Channel, and the Sci-Fi Channel, didn't seem all that exciting. Bigfoot doesn't have the charm of the Loch Ness Monster and certainly doesn't scare Americans quite like an alien abduction. I agreed with her that my topic was a bit off the beaten path. However, my experience as a child with Grandpa in the West Virginia woods stuck with me. It's possible that a pissed-off, and quite possibly horny, Bigfoot chased Grandpa and me in 1980.

I started jotting notes for this book between 2004 and 2007 — first as a collection of thoughts on individuals that follow Bigfoot. When telling stories to others about my downright mind-blowing adventures tracking my favorite mythological beast, friends, family, and strangers began to volunteer information about their Bigfoot beliefs and experiences. It was then I began to write about something else entirely — a book about those who believe and what those beliefs encompass.

I worked in the National Security Agency (NSA), the very same organization that chased Will Smith and Gene Hackman in *Enemy of the State*. My wife and I own an internationally acclaimed distillery called "Silverback" in the Blue Ridge Mountains of Virginia. I am currently a Representative in the United States Congress, elected in 2018. (Note: I added this tidbit of political information just before publishing because my opponent in the Congressional race, Leslie Cockburn, accused me of being a Bigfoot Erotica "devotee". I do not dabble in monster porn, although my wife does call me her Silverback. However, I am now intrigued by Bigfoot Erotica and will get to the *bottom* of the matter. How could someone kink-shame those gentle souls who take delight in the soulful, passionate moan of Sasquatch? Cockburn's own beliefs align with those that worship Bigfoot as an inter-dimensional superhero). I started and sold a wildly successful Department of Defense contracting company that specialized in intelligence analysis. No, I am not a spy, and I try not to listen in when you call 1-900-LUV-GALS or GUYS. Before my stint in the NSA, I served as an intelligence officer in the United States Air Force. Right up front, I'll confess that I do not believe in the probability of Bigfoot. However, intelligence professionals distinguish between *probability* and *possibility*. It's *possible* that Osama Bin Laden was your next-door neighbor and tended his garden in the nude, but it's not *probable*. Bigfoot is a *possibility*. That being said, the story of my grandpa in the first chapter is completely true. My grandpa was a most honest man. I was ten years old when something chased my grandfather and me. But my views on Bigfoot hold no moral tale. I'm a Bigfoot nihilist. As my research deepened, and I was exposed to many true believers, my book morphed into a research project more about Bigfoot Believers than Bigfoot.

I decided right off that I needed to look for my hairy friend. Searching for Bigfoot with experts would educate me about reported Bigfoot habits and allow me to assimilate research "language" needed to present Bigfoot and his merry followers in a credible way. I investigated the internet for the perfect Bigfoot expedition, using a keyword search, and stumbled upon an organization that impressed me with a professional website, sighting database, and research articles.

For my first Bigfoot expedition, I chose a weekend that coincided with my wedding anniversary. I thought it would be a hoot to take my wife and best friend, Steve Spinner (hereafter referred to only as "Spinner"), along on a camping adventure. I contacted the Bigfoot expedition coordinator. We talked at length about the Bigfoot mystery, even though he seemed apprehensive when I informed him about my in-process Bigfoot book and my military background. His suspicion could probably be chalked up to my occupation as a Department of Defense intelligence analyst. At the end of our conversation, he insisted that I sign a confidentiality agreement.

Now, *I* was suspicious, but I agreed to pay the two thousand dollars he asked for … a discount from the three thousand he originally quoted. When I'm suspicious, I'm curious. Why the secrecy? Why the paranoia? My motive for attending this expedition was so innocent that I could not comprehend why the expedition leader/coordinator thought it necessary that I should sign a confidentiality agreement.

My wife, Spinner, and I flew to Washington State one month later.

This is an adult adventure book, a sordid travel book for those weary of the usual fare. Bigfoot Believers exist. They work beside you. Some pray to a mystical Bigfoot as guardian of inter-dimensional portals. Others are convinced that Bigfoot uses psychic attacks or infrasound to paralyze campers and other outdoor unfortunates. Others think Bigfoot talks to them … in English … through ESP. Many believe Bigfoot communicates in a language called "samurai" and can't speak English at all. Women believers theorize about Bigfoot's penis size and proportionality. Some believe Bigfoot has gluten allergies and shouldn't be baited with peanut butter and jelly sandwiches. And there are those special believers who think Bigfoot awareness is best accomplished through chest-thumping sex with other believers.

I've roasted marshmallows with the believers. I've read their books. I've interviewed them. I've broke bread with them. They talk in reverential awe about Bigfoot, Sasquatch, Oh-Mah, and Stick People. Bigfoot's flesh is sacred. He is a protector. He is above mere mortals. He is to be written about. He is to be worshipped. He is to be studied exhaustively, from his eating habits to his mating habits.

And so goes this tale about true believers who see Bigfoot as simply an evolutionary miracle--- and for all those others who worship at the altar of their Hirsute God.

Monsters are real. I've talked with them. I've turned down their advances.

A DISCUSSION ON SIMIAN GENITALIA

Before I get into the "meat" of this incredibly fascinating book, I need to desensitize you, the reader, to a concept that could be uncomfortable. Now, that Bigfoot Erotica is part of the discussion (Thank you, congressional opponent) all of us must be open-minded.

Apparently, Bigfoot is spectacularly endowed.

I want to apologize to all Bigfoot believers who are quite sure that Bigfoot is an ape. He isn't. Apes have very small genitalia. Bigfoot is a man, baby. Or something close to man.

EATEN BY THE MIGHTY PECULIAR

I ran away from a monster when I was ten years old.

My family owned one hundred forty-three acres just outside Petersburg, West Virginia, a little depressed hamlet famous for being "Home of the Golden Trout." Our property was a steep, almost unusable track of ravines and mountain land that bordered the Monongahela National Forest. Hogs and cattle had fed on the ragged mountainsides for decades. My great-grandmother lived in the hollow of the property, inside a wood-sided house built by relatives in the 1930s. Every other weekend we visited to take my great-grandmother, called Nana, to the store and to do work. We built fences, hoed potatoes, cut grass, fixed the road, painted barns, shot groundhogs, and picked apples. My grandparents and I did not stay with Nana in her cat-infested house. None of us appreciated the odor of cat feces on the newspaper-covered couch and easy chair. We slept in a hunting trailer on top of our mountain. At night, I sat on the rough-hewn porch that my grandfather built and marveled at the twinkling lights in the valley below. It was as if civilization ended on the outskirts of town. One step outside the artificial light and wolves would attack, or inebriated, inbred rednecks with crazy eyes and rotted teeth would kidnap me for unseemly purposes. Maybe female vampires in bikinis, blood dripping from razor-sharp fangs, would fly in during a full moon and carry me off. At ten years old, I thought that last fantasy particularly enticing.

It was early November 1980, only weeks before the opening of deer season. We decided to take a jaunt to Bulls Head, a mountaintop spring that provided cattle and other animals with water. Years before, a consortium of landowners from the top of the mountain down to the valley below had decided to tap the Bulls Head spring so that cattle, sheep, goats, and horses could water regularly. The farmers built an amazingly long and effective steel piping system that would open and dump water into troughs positioned at regular intervals along the route. This pipe was called the "Spring Line."

From our rough-hewn porch, the arduous hike to Bulls Head took approximately one hour. We would follow the Spring Line. If we hustled, Grandpa and I should arrive back at the trailer before dark. Just in time to roast a few marshmallows.

Darkness did not bother me. Even with fantasies of ghouls (goolies) floating about in my noggin, our family land provided safe shelter. Deer, turkeys, groundhogs, snakes, and an occasional bear were as familiar to me as my own living room. Often, I would stay out alone well after sunset, sitting on a stump and listening to the night. Whippoorwills and frogs sang to me.

Usually when we hiked to the Bulls Head, Grandpa carried a 30-30 rifle. He didn't this time. He carried a knife, as always. I later wondered what would have happened if Grandpa had decided to take the rifle along. Would we be famous? Or rich? Or dead?

We began our walk. A few hundred yards up from the trailer, we unlatched and walked through the boundary gate that separated our property from those higher on the mountain. After closing the gate, we stopped for a few moments. The Spring Line paralleled the logging road that wound through all the properties. On this side of the boundary gate, a huge meadow stretched to where the road and Spring Line disappeared into the trees. We waited, because deer sometimes fed in this area. No deer today.

"Let's go," said Grandpa. He was like the grandpas of storybooks. His deep bass voice rumbled in his chest. He feared no man. He could shoot the nuts off a mosquito at two hundred yards. He could hoe potatoes and castrate hogs. He fixed machinery and fried perfect eggs. He drank Old Milwaukee beer and played poker. He was the governor of the local Moose Lodge. And, he could spot a deer before anyone else. His piercing gaze penetrated the woolliest bush, the dimmest dusk.

We kept a steady pace, knowing exactly how fast we needed to go to complete the hike before dark.

"There," said Grandpa. He pointed at a spot in front and above us.

"I don't see any deer," I said.

"Look above the three trees growing together," said Grandpa.

I stared for seconds, a minute, and then slowly a brown spot emerged, a doe munching on undergrowth, unaware that two predators watched her from a hundred yards away. My grandfather didn't need binoculars. He knew every crag, every twist, every roll, every tree and plant for miles. He had been raised in these mountains.

4

We walked and watched deer. I ran ahead of him. I thought that maybe I could spot a deer before he did. I never succeeded. He always found the animals first and then smiled with quiet contentment. His ability to spot animals amazed me. I wanted to be just like him. He taught me how to look for deer, to notice movement, to stare *through* the trees and not *at* the trees. Slightly bow-legged, his effortless gait pushed him along surprisingly fast. My young lungs strained to keep up when he really got going, but I never complained.

Time is magnificently deceptive during youth. The hike to Bulls Head took forever and no time at all. I dropped to my knees when we reached the spring, cupped my hands and scooped the arctic cold water to my mouth. I wrapped my hand around the frosted pipe, gasped at its coldness and imagined how far it penetrated the mountain. Spring water spilled into the depression around the pipe, the beginnings of a continuous running stream.

Grandpa drank too. Satiated with spring water, we sat on rocks surrounding Bulls Head and from our high perch stared into the blue haze of the Appalachians. Just hundreds of yards behind us, the dark and magnificent Monongahela National Forest waited with hushed expectation. I burped. Rocks and boulders surrounding us were pitted with fossils. Dead for eons, extinct since the dinosaurs, imprinted forever. I traced their outlines with my finger.

Grandpa and I played the game we always played when we hiked. We would search for heavy, round rocks and heave them down the slope that bordered the logging road. We would count how many seconds it took for each rock to reach bottom, the rock's descent echoing across the peaks as it slammed into trees, stumps and brush—a crashing, banging cacophony. We played the game as we walked back toward the trailer. That day, no wind blew through the mountains, and as the sun set and the rocks crashed, I remember wincing.

With what happened only minutes later, I wonder if the noise from those rolling rocks piqued the curiosity of something else entirely.

Darker now. Colder, too. The sun falling slowly under the horizon, but the top half still visible through gaps in the mountains. We reached our boundary gate. Grandpa didn't unlatch the gate but stared back down the logging road. We had stopped our boulder-heaving and hoped for one last whitetail sighting.

"Hear that?" asked Grandpa.

I shook my head. *Nope.*

Grandpa hopped onto a high stump outside the gate. He peered up into the mountain laurel that bordered this part of the road. Even this close to winter, the green shiny leaves of the mountain laurel reflected the last remaining sun rays, making it difficult to make out any animals in the undergrowth.

A loud crash exploded only one hundred yards above us, and I almost pissed myself. It was louder than a rolling boulder.

"I hear it now," I whispered to Grandpa.

He waved his hand at me, the international sign for *shut up*. Grandpa peered into the brush unblinking, silent. Was it a bear? A flock of turkeys? A buck in rut?

Another crash. Closer still. Grandpa bent over, trying to see *through* the laurel. I waited behind him and below him. I couldn't see around him, and to either side the shiny mountain laurel leaves blinded me. I wished that the sun would hurry and set all the way.

"Run," said Grandpa. His tone was matter-of-fact.

For an instant I thought I heard him wrong. I didn't move. Run? Why? To where?

Grandpa jumped from the stump. He grabbed my shoulders and stared into my eyes.

"Run," said Grandpa again.

Another crash almost on top of us. I turned, stumbled the ten yards to the boundary fence. I struggled to climb the gate. Panic. I didn't think to unlatch it; I felt hands round my waist and then I flew over the gate and tumbled onto the road below. I rolled to my back. He had already climbed to the top of the gate. He didn't yell. His boots thudded on the hard-pack when he landed beside my head. He jerked me upright.

"Run," he said, louder this time.

I kicked in the afterburners. I ran like Satan himself chased me. I ran because Grandpa was already making tracks down the mountain toward our trailer two hundred and fifty yards away. Even with my thrusters on full, I could barely keep up with the old man.

Crash. Grandpa glanced up and to his left.

It followed us. It *chased* us. *Don't fall, don't fall.* So much momentum as we rushed pell-mell toward safety, arms pinwheeling for balance. Falling at this speed would result in serious rock rash and possible broken bones. The monster would get me.

Crash.

Our green and white trailer visible through the trees, on

the front porch, Grandpa's 30–30 lever action leaned against a chair. Inside the trailer, Grandpa kept a .22 rimfire in the closet.

The trailer. Safety. Although the door lock was simply an eye-hook, at least we had weapons inside and the ability to control the threat's point of entry, only one door. The lime-green trailer was four hundred square feet small.

Grandpa reached the porch just ahead of me. I gasped, a combination of physical exertion and panic zapping my oxygen reserves. He grabbed the 30–30 off the porch. He checked the breech to make sure it was loaded. It was.

"Get the .22," said Grandpa. I went inside, pushed a shell into the chamber, and then joined him on the porch.

Grandpa stood at the porch stairs. He stared intently into the woods, *through* the woods. About fifty yards of weeds, brush, and fallen trees separated the wood line from the barbed-wire fence surrounding the back "yard." Nothing wild or supernatural could traverse those fifty yards without Grandpa seeing and shooting whatever he saw. I stood behind him, .22 rifle pointed at the ground. Even at the age of ten I realized that a rimfire would have little effect on any animal larger than a groundhog. But the feel of a rifle in my hands comforted me. I took even more comfort in the fact that Grandpa stood out front with an infinitely more powerful weapon.

We waited. We watched. Five minutes. Ten minutes. Only when listening for danger does one realize how quiet the late-autumn forest can be. Every noise explodes in the quiet—a squirrel jumping from a fallen log, a cawing crow, leaves rustling in the freshening breeze, the faint rattling of a propeller driven airplane, my own breathing and pounding in the temples. I expected the mystery animal to emerge from the dark woods any moment, charging us with a lumbering gait and dripping fangs. Grandpa would open up on the beast, working the lever action like a Wild West sheriff.

Almost completely dark. Grandpa sighed and turned around. I stiffened.

"Are you hungry?" he asked.

I relaxed. "Yes."

Grandpa watched the woods for thirty seconds more. No loud crash. No charging beast.

"Let's eat," he said. He patted my shoulder and marched past me to the trailer door. I stood by myself, .22 in hand, and stared into the gloom.

"Coming in?"

"What was it?"

"Don't know." Grandpa shrugged. "Nothing to worry about now."

I wondered why he still held his 30-30 at the ready. I wondered if he lied to me. Because it damn sure felt like there was still something to worry about.

Not long ago, I interviewed my grandfather about that day forty years ago. He admitted that he saw a large, dark animal. He couldn't identify the animal, only that it seemed "mighty peculiar." When I was ten years old I believed in the "Mighty Peculiar" enough so that when I watched an episode of *In Search Of* about Bigfoot and saw for the first time the Patterson-Gimlin film about Bigfoot, I automatically concluded that the "Mighty Peculiar" that chased me in 1980 only could have been Sasquatch. And that Sasquatch sounded like Leonard Nimoy.

BIGFOOT'S HOTDOG

Olympic National Forest, Washington State, 2004…not far from Kalaloch Lodge.

"Is it 1:00 a.m. yet?" I asked.

"Almost," my buddy whispered.

"Hear anything?"

"Not with you talking."

The sound of drops hitting my Gore-Tex shell sounded like pebbles striking a tarp.

"Jesus," my buddy whispered. "That's fucking loud."

I questioned myself for the tenth time. Why was I sitting here in the dark three thousand miles from home? I felt like Charlie Sheen in *Platoon* after he awoke to ants biting his face. Leaves released leftover raindrops that splattered in the undergrowth. Only an hour before, the downpour had stopped, but the thick canopy leaked the downpour's remainder on us. The sky had cleared, but the growth above us obscured stars, moon, and light. Flying bugs landed on every exposed piece of skin. Keeping still was almost impossible. We sat sixty feet above the swampy access to a river full of salmon, both dead and alive. I sat on a wet stump, my buddy Spinner crouched beside me. Our eyes watered from the stink of rotting fish. Around us tall firs, scraggly brush, and impenetrable vine created a black wall of unknowing. The Motorola walkie-talkie shook in my hands, one of those cheap family radio band models. My earpiece crackled with static. A voice occasionally interrupted the static, telling us to stay calm, that if It – the creature – splashed below us in the river, It wouldn't hurt us.

The voice belonged to the expedition leader (EL).

Spinner scanned the darkness with a Gen 1 Bushnell night-vision device. He saw fuzzy outlines and indiscernible blobs. We resisted the impulse to use the infrared illuminator (IR). Experts hypothesized that the creature could see IR, that a beam invisible to the naked human eye would appear as a spotlight to It. Next time, if I search for a mythical beast again, I sure as hell will purchase a Gen-3 night-vision device. Not just to see It, but to see if a hungry bear might be waiting close, licking its paws and wondering why two dumb-ass humans are sitting on the side of the hill above a river scanning the forest with a piece-of-junk Gen 1. Above us on the logging road, a half-dozen fellow adventurers waited with breathless anticipation for our report on It.

Maybe our *final* report.

Waiting for our screams.

My wife was with them. I'm sure she giggled.

"I'm using the IR," said Spinner. "I hear something down there, and I'll be goddamned if I'm going to let it sneak up on us."

"Could be what we seek," I intoned. Like a preacher.

Spinner chuckled. "Or a bear." He depressed the button on the side. He scanned left to right slowly.

"Anything?"

"No," said Spinner. "I can see maybe ten feet."

"They say It stinks…like rotting fish, or farts," I said. "Smells like a bit of both in here."

"I farted," said Spinner.

"That explains it then," I said. We both started to giggle, in that hysterical *what the hell are we doing out here* way. I held my stomach and put the radio up to my mouth. I could barely contain the wailing scream of laughter working its way up my windpipe. And my ass was so *wet* from the stump. Hysteria results from many things. It wasn't only the ridiculousness of our situation, it was the worm crawling about in my gut called fear. Maybe a missing link did roam, eat, and mate in the Pacific Northwest. Maybe the true believers surrounding us this night were the apostles of a new discovery. No one in their right mind would be in the middle of the wilderness, next to a river, during the salmon run, in bear country, looking for Bigfoot.

But here I was. A former NSA employee and military officer sitting next to a decorated state trooper scanning the forest with obsolete equipment, holding a cheap radio to my ear, wincing at rain smacking my Gore-Tex, and trying to maneuver my backside so that my wet underwear wouldn't ride up my crack.

Jesus.

And, we didn't have a firearm.

Stupid.

Spinner fell in the leaves, trying to giggle in silence.

We finally contained our hysterics, small snorts and fits ending in exhausted sniffling and wiping of eyes. We attempted to regain composure.

"Man, it got quiet." Spinner quickly began scanning again with the Gen 1.

Like a tomb. Where was the dripping water? The rustling leaves?

"Ready to go?" asked Spinner.

I was ready. I nodded in the darkness, went to pat Spinner on the shoulder. *Crack.* Like a bat hitting a baseball, an explosion of sound no more than sixty feet below us.

I mouthed, "Holy ... hell."

Spinner and I stared at one another in the darkness. My earpiece crackled again. The voice said, "It's coming closer. Do you hear it?"

I keyed the radio twice. I was not going to verbalize.

"Stay still," the voice said. "It won't hurt you."

What won't hurt me? A bear? An elk? A deer? Bigfoot? Maybe the Loch Ness monster had swum up this particular river all the way from Scotland.

Spinner shook his head. "A falling branch, that's all," he whispered. "Or a deer."

I whispered into the radio, "Probably an animal, but something's down there."

"Does it stink?" asked the voice.

"Yes," I whispered. "Like dead fish."

"He's close then," said the voice. "Bigfoot smells like rotting fish."

And I thought that rotting fish smelled like rotting fish. Silly me. But, I would be lying if I said I wasn't terrified. I even hypothesized that since Bigfoot smelled like rotting fish that Bigfoot hung around rotting fish so that no one would know that he was around, a rotting fish camouflage, or *stinkaflage.*

Another loud crack. Further away, almost like it was on the other side of the river now.

14

I reported the noise and my impression that it sounded like it moved.

"Maybe more than one Bigfoot in there," said the voice. "They could be communicating with each other, reporting your location."

"Great," I whispered back. "Just great."

Spinner snickered.

"Ain't it a rush?" said the voice. "The first time is always the scariest. Just stay calm. They won't hurt you."

"He says they won't hurt us," I said to Spinner. "Just stay calm."

"They?" asked Spinner. "Like, more than one?"

"Yeah," I said.

"Bullshit," said Spinner. "There's no such thing as Bigfoot."

"It's so dark in here," I said.

Another voice whispered in my earpiece. It wasn't the voice of the EL, but the voice of a Native American Bigfoot tracker that Spinner and I had befriended earlier during the expedition introductions. Our Yakama pal believed in Bigfoot unconditionally.

"I'm coming in," said our Yakama friend in his monotone bass voice.

So even in our terror we waited for our Native American friend. We listened to the squeal of the radio, the dripping water, the intermittent clicks and scuffles of live animals or other unknown things making noise. And, finally we heard the unmistakable footfalls of a bipedal creature scuffling on the other side of the ridge. It was our Yakama buddy, Mel.

"Nothing over here, fellas," said Mel over his Motorola. "Looks like some elk tracks on this trail." Through the thick, we spotted stray beams shooting from Mel's flashlight. "No bear tracks, but even with the flashlight, I can't see much." He waved the light back and forth. "Let's go to another location."

"No sign of Bigfoot, then?" I talked normally now, unafraid on the Motorola. Other people were in the forest.

"Can never rule it out," said Mel. He was hesitant. "No sign, though."

The voice of the EL cut across our channel. "I know he was there. Don't second-guess yourselves. It's a thrill—right, guys?"

Spinner flipped on his flashlight and held it under his chin, illuminating his face. Then he rolled his eyes.

"Time to go," I said.

"There's no damn Bigfoot."

"You weren't scared? Even a little bit?"

"Worried about bears." Spinner stood. He reached down, grabbed his ruck, and threw it over his shoulders. He cinched the straps tight. "That nut case up there wants us to believe Bigfoot was down here."

"Maybe he was." I shrugged. I clicked on my head lamp.

"Did you drink the Bigfoot Kool-Aid?" asked Spinner.

I smiled. "I think you were scared."

"I think you're full of shit."

"Probably am. You leading us out of here, or what?"

Spinner, my wife, and I sat around a campfire with a half dozen others, roasting marshmallows. Around us, excited jabbering about the night's events flowed between those who reported some type of Bigfoot experience and those who dearly wished that they'd had the opportunity to see or hear or smell or *sense* Bigfoot. Many of those talking were Bigfoot expedition virgins, like me, trading hypotheses on the likelihood of Bigfoot's existence like mad scientists. They opined on everything Bigfoot, about whether It was mystical, a magic being that traveled between dimensions like an otherworldly long jumper, or whether It was simply a biological anomaly, a missing link that humans could research.

"Could be just a hairy man," said one participant. He wiped marshmallow goo from his beard.

"No way," said a shrill female. "Bigfoot can sense us. He's more attracted to females than males."

That caught my wife's attention, although barely. I had been with Christine since just after my sixteenth birthday.

"Why do you think Bigfoot is attracted to females?"

"Well, I've seen Bigfoot on numerous occasions," said the female.

So, Bigfoot is attracted just to *you*?" asked Christine.

"No, three of the girls have seen him. Even sketched what they saw."

Mel had joined us by this time. I offered him a hot dog on a stick. He politely declined with a wave of his hand and sat down beside me on a fold-out chair.

"You have drawings?" I heard my wife ask, slightly incredulous.

"I saw two at one time," said the female. "Looking at me from behind a tree." She inhaled deeply, her eyes alight with remembrance. "A life-changing experience."

"Wow," I said. My marshmallow turned perfectly brown. I pulled it from the flames just before it melted off the stick.

17

I then started scalding a hot dog. If Mel didn't want the hot dog, it was all mine.

Mel said, "An old lady living deep in the reservation says they come to her home every month. She saw a large male during daylight."

"How tall?" asked Spinner.

"She told me its head touched the bottom limb of a large tree in her yard. From the ground to the bottom of the limb measured nine feet. A very large male."

"Easy to figure out it was male?" asked Christine.

"Sure," said Mel. "She could tell." He glanced at me for moral support. I shrugged.

"Was he proportionate?" asked the female that sketched. She was itching to draw another picture.

"What's going on here?" I waved the hot dog on the stick in the air. "You girls want to know the size of Bigfoot's pecker?"

"Of course," said Christine. "Every woman wants to know. Is Bigfoot's penis proportionate? I mean, how big was it?"

"Yeah," said the girl that sketched.

Mel squirmed in the chair. "It was proportionate." He held his hands apart as if measuring a fish.

"That's a foot long," said Spinner. "At least."

"Damn," said Christine.

We all looked at her. Some guys from Texas were there too.

"You guys can't tell me that you're not curious too?" asked Christine to us and the Texans.

The men were silent for a spell. Then almost in unison we all mumbled sheepishly, "Yeah. We wanna know."

The girl who sketched stared at Mel's hands. Her face

flushed. If she had a fan, she would have waved it back and forth to cool herself. "Amazing," she finally said.

Around us, others conversed about Bigfoot. Many drank beer or wine from a box. Laughter erupted here and there, guffaws and wailings of the inebriated or almost-inebriated. I watched the expedition leader make his rounds, visiting every campfire. Many asked the EL questions pertaining to Bigfoot diet, habits, range, mating behavior, language, and population densities. He had a ready answer to every question, confident pronouncements on the what, where, when, why, and how of Bigfoot, a walking crypto-zoological encyclopedia. As the night grew late, man and woman pairs stumbled back to their tents. Many arrived at the expedition sans significant other, leaving spouses, girlfriends and boyfriends at home. Some did participate as couples, like Christine and me. But it did seem odd that some slept in tents other than their own … and that some that we had met mentioned that they left their significant others at home … and those individuals had rapidly established an intimate rapport with other Bigfoot believers.

Females surrounded the expedition leader. Eventually the girl who sketched left our campfire to join the other females. It was close to dawn. Fires flickered out.

I drank a beer.

Spinner, Christine, and I were left alone.

Spinner said, "Wow."

"Uh-huh," I said.

"Crazy night," said Christine.

We roasted the last of the hot dogs and marshmallows.

FUNKY MONKEY BUBBLE GUM

Spinner stayed in the room with my wife and me at Kalaloch Lodge. Counting airfare, lodging, food, gas, incidentals, and a rental car, I estimated that I would drop between five and six thousand dollars on this Bigfoot expedition. Only our first night of three and I felt like the world's biggest sucker. I sat on the edge of the bed and contemplated our experience.

This wasn't eco-tourism or adventure camping. I had paid massive scratch to tramp around public land with "scouts" who proclaimed unique knowledge, and they had none.

For some reason, I thought that the money I paid—four thousand for the expedition alone—should have at least gotten me a lousy t-shirt with a crappy artist's rendition of Bigfoot.

Nope. During our first morning of Bigfoot "education" seminars, which lasted all of fifteen minutes, I stared with wide-eyed and slack-jawed wonder while a military reservist showed us Bigfoot virgins how to measure Bigfoot tracks with a four-foot walking stick. While the other participants in the expedition party expressed unabashed wonderment at the reservist's tracking acumen, Spinner, Christine, and I stifled laughter and inappropriate comments.

Another Bigfoot expedition veteran played a CD of Bigfoot "language," a guttural Asian-sounding dialect interspersed with ear-splitting howls, high-pitched chattering, and random whistles.

"If you hear that," said the veteran, "a Bigfoot is close by, trying to communicate with you. We call this language *Samurai*."

"I call that my first girlfriend in the sack," said Spinner.

"If I hear that," I said, "I'm shooting it."

"Don't shoot my girlfriend," said Spinner.

It all seemed so god-damned ludicrous.

Now, Spinner lay on his back staring at the ceiling. My wife sat beside me, quiet. No doubt, they were as confused as I about what we'd paid for.

"Bigfoot is a sex machine," said Spinner through clenched teeth. "Him and his massive pecker."

"I expected more than this," I said.

"Sorry, man." Spinner sat up now. "It's a great lodge. Beautiful beach. You picked a great spot."

"Most of the others are staying at the campground, tent swapping," I said. "It's a social club."

"We're having a good time, honey." My wife patted my knee. "It's almost morning. I'm going to bed."

"Me too," said Spinner. "Long day tomorrow."

Spinner drifted off to sleep. Then my wife. I lay next to her, listening to her breathe. I should have passed out too, after the all-night vigil amongst the rotting fish, the hiking, the flight cross county from Pennsylvania to Seattle, the jet lag.

I couldn't sleep. I quietly rolled out of bed. I opened the door, slowly. I slipped into the night. Dawn couldn't be more than an hour away. A cigarette would be appropriate now. It would at least give me a reason to stand outside my hotel door. People never questioned the lone man smoking a cigarette in an alley. It was simply appropriate. *My, he's a mighty decent fellow. He's just burning a fag on the landing.*

But I didn't smoke.

Wind whistled in from the oceanside, rustling the tall firs encircling the lodge. The green wall surrounding me swayed and sighed. Closing my eyes, I listened. Just inside my room I had a working toilet, heat, and air conditioning. Just on the other side of those sighing trees, a monster could be spying on the lodge. Not so hard to believe that monsters roamed the woods when the wind blew, and the moon snuck behind clouds. Swift darkness; a chill worked its way down my spine. I opened my eyes, imagining a hirsute man beast exploding from the tree-line, loping toward me through the penumbra of the dim parking-lot streetlights. There's a lure to Bigfoot, a mystery, a missing link, a belief that something greater than ourselves does exist *out there*. The search for meaning in this life is addictive, as is the need to belong. Everyone believes they hold secrets to eternity. The Catholic priest, the Muslim imam, the Protestant clergy, the Democrats, the Republicans, the Green Party, David Koresh, Jim Jones, Al Gore, Heaven's Gate Cult members and their magic mystery ride on Hale-Bopp. Belief systems to manipulate the manipulables .

On the second-floor landing above me I heard a door open and then close, a furtive click. I smelled cigarette smoke, and then listened as footfalls crossed above me and onto the stairs that descended to a spot directly beside my room, next to the soda machine and snack dispenser. I stepped back into the shadows of the hotel door so fast I almost banged my heels against the stoop. What was I afraid of? I wasn't breaking any laws.

Down the stairs. A man immediately turned left, passing by the soda and snack machines. I held my breath. No movement or he might spot me. He walked with a purpose, like he was late for work. His shirt flopped around his waistband, his hair mussed, disheveled. His boots were untied. He opened the driver's door of his older-model Chevrolet and slipped in. He started the car as soon as he sat down and in one motion shut the door and reversed out of the parking space.

He was in a hurry.

He never looked back, never did anything but keep his head ramrod-straight until he reversed. His brake lights barely brightened when he made the right-hand turn to leave the parking lot. A slight squeal of tires, and he was gone.

I had recognized the guy, had talked to him during the Bigfoot education seminars. He stayed in a tent at the campground, alone, one of the Bigfoot expedition veterans. He had told me, "My wife hates it when I go on these trips." He laughed, clapped me on the back.

Alone again I emerged from the shadows, just me, the sighing firs, and the Bigfoot that might appear any moment. If I had a cig, I would have lit it, slowly inhaling and then leaning over the rail bolted to the narrow concrete porch that ran the whole length of the bottom floor. The moon appeared again--not much of a moon, but bright enough to comfort me.

HALE-BOPP
IS HOT BETWEEN MY LEGS

It's no wonder that truth is stranger than fiction.
Fiction has to make sense.

-Mark Twain

The following morning, I sat opposite a fine East Coast fellow at the Kalaloch Lodge breakfast table. He and his teenage son shoveled pancakes into their mouths and excitedly talked of the prior night's events. Most of those events involved Spinner, me, a crashing noise, and rotting fish. Spinner and I tried to downplay the prior evening, assuring him and his son that we did not encounter Bigfoot. More likely, a large animal like a bear or deer had crossed in front of us during the night. The rotting fish smell turned out to be rotting fish. No surprises, no chance at all that a surreptitious Gigantopithecus Blacki stalked us in the night. Hell, even if Bigfoot had come a-calling, our cheap Generation-1 night-vision scope would have missed it.

The man--I'll call him Chuck--said, "Bigfoot exists. I know it." He tapped his chest with his finger, right over his heart. "This doesn't lie."

Christine, eating an omelet beside me, said, "Feelings can lie."

"Ever seen it, Chuck?" asked Spinner.

"No," said the man. "I just know it! Evidence is overwhelming. Check out the internet. All kinds of sightings and facts."

The internet does have interesting facts. I agreed with Chuck on that. Google "Bigfoot" tonight. See what your search brings up. Google "Psychic Bigfoot". Google "Bigfoot and wormhole". Google "Warlock". Google "Spirit Portals". Google "Energy Beings". Google "Project Blue Book". Google "Mothman". Google "Loch Ness Monster". Google "Amway". Google "Team of Destiny". Google "Democrats save America". Google "Republicans save America". Google every belief or political system you can think of. Google "Truth Revolution". Google "KKK". Google "Black Panthers". Google "Satanism". Google "Wicca". Google "QAnon". Google "Jim Jones and Guyana". Google "Auras". Google "Indigo Children". Google "Alien Abduction". Google "Heaven's Gate". Google "Traditionalist Workers Party."

Many of the websites you find will espouse the rightness of a cause, belief, idea, or being. Some will explain how that belief or cause turned tragic for some. Many websites are created by those whom I believe to be paranoid, neurotic, criminal, greedy, misguided, ignorant, gullible, or plain psychopathic. Fiction is fantasy. Non-fiction can thrust you and me into lunacy. The stuff below is real…to someone. It all resides on our information highway called the internet:

Don't drink the Kool-Aid!
The Bigfoot body is still in the vortex of the wormhole!
Find out if your new baby is an Indigo Child!

Mohammed can kiss my ass!

Mothman is a truly paranormal cryptozoological creature!

Positive programming is the way to persuade others! The power of positive inspiration!

Crystal Children began appearing on the planet in the year 2000!

Shadow beings exist on the edge of our peripheral vision!

I have the key to multi-dimensional consciousness!

Bashar is a multi-dimensional being!

Then a probe was inserted in my anus!

Save America! Vote Republican!

The Nagas tribe dwells in the Snake-World under the Himalayas!

Save America! Vote Democrat!

The People's Temple was an experimental laboratory operated by the CIA!

Mary Magdalene seduced Jesus!

Mothman chased a Red Cross Bloodmobile!

The ritual of realization summons the daemon!

The law is sacred!

The Alpha-Draconians do not want us to attain interstellar capabilities!

Grandma's Wicca "energy" secrets discovered inside a trunk!

#WWG1WGA!

Do beings in the fourth dimension have teeth?

Ernesto "Che" Guevara was a great revolutionary!

Your aura can be weakened by using crack!

IDB strands for "Inter-Dimensional Being!"

Have you hugged your IDB today!

I won the orb viewer war!

Attention Deficit Disorder is a common misdiagnosis for Indigo Children!

Wiccans practice their rituals skyclad (naked) inside their magic circle!

Before Heaven's Gate there was HIM – Human Individual Metamorphosis!

Chuck was a good man, intelligent and financially successful. We all liked him. This didn't stop Spinner, Christine, and me from staring at him in mid-chew, unable to comprehend his belief in Bigfoot based entirely on gut feeling, internet research, and the inspirational words from the Bigfoot expedition leader.

"Faith," said Chuck. He waved his fork at us, a piece of syrup-slimed pancake impaled on its end. "We're going to find Bigfoot." To be fair, Chuck smiled, and I think he was joking a little.

Chuck's "Bigfoot faith statement" made as much sense to me as: *The Alpha-Draconians do not want us to attain interstellar capabilities!*

But faith led Chuck to believe that on the morrow, or that night even, someone in the search party would find evidence of his gigantic friend. Whether a sound, a footprint, a smell, a feeling (the sixth sense!) or a sighting, Bigfoot would reveal himself to those who truly searched. Too many clues had been left over the years to discount the notion that Bigfoot could be imagination or hoax.

"Think of the prints," Chuck said. "No one would or could fake some five-toed footprint miles from civilization. Some of those are real, I know it."

We nodded at him. We continued to eat and listen.

"So many sightings." Chuck sipped his coffee. "Not all

hallucinated. Impossible." He laughed with a sure chuckle and a twinkle in his eyes. His mustache twitched. "Doctors, lawyers, soldiers, professionals. They can't all be crazy!"

We shrugged with mute acquiescence, muttered in unison *not everyone could be crazy.*

Rain started to fall. Maybe the rain had never ended, only increased in intensity. I sat closest to the window, enjoyed the rat-a-tat-tat of drops striking the window despite my reservations about tramping about the Hoh rainforest later that night. The Kalaloch Lodge restaurant was perched on a bluff overlooking the Pacific. I stared at the beach, once again marveling at the trees jumbled on the sand like colossal petrified carcasses. Some of the trees measured fifty feet from root to tip. A few brave souls walked their dogs among the dead giants, Lilliputians gallivanting amongst petrified Gullivers. Three pairs of contemplative tourists wearing waterproof windbreakers sat in the sand, allowing seawater to lick their toes while they studied the horizon.

I wanted to believe Chuck. Spinner wanted to believe him. Christine wanted to believe him, especially if the Bigfoot happened to be male so that she could catch a glimpse of the ample hose-like beasthood described, via Mel, by the aged Native American lady from the reservation.

I continued to stare at the people on the beach while Chuck gobbled his hotcakes. Weren't we all the same, really, Lilliputians looking for Gulliver, whether that Gulliver be hirsute and supernaturally endowed, or just plain supernatural? Appetite gone, I waited patiently for the rest to finish. Chuck finished first, grabbed his Indiana Jones hat, and bid us farewell.

"See you at camp," said Chuck. "To a successful hunt." He gave us tidy salute. We half-heartedly waved back.

I paid the check with a credit card.

Breakfast finished, we walked back in the hard drizzle to our lodge room. The rain did not drive the dog-walkers or horizon-watchers away, because in Washington State this weather was the norm. My grandfather called this kind of rain a "spit" --intermittent downpours followed by misting, drizzle, and then another furious few seconds of blowing rain. Not entirely unpleasant, almost appropriate for the landscape, this lush rough green bordering a tree graveyard on the edge of the Pacific. A balmy, breezy day would soften the severity of the beach, of the windswept firs bordering the lodge. None of us wanted it softened. Its peculiar loneliness connected us all, reminded us that insignificance is not such a bad thing. Cleansing almost, a reality check for those caught up in a world where the single most important decision in a day is whether to take the train or drive into work. Balmy and breezy wouldn't satisfy me here on this bluff.

This adventure, although fun in many ways, had become oppressive. I couldn't fathom anyone stumbling upon some incontrovertible Bigfoot truth in three to four days of searching among thirty or forty so-called believers. Hell, some of the Bigfoot disciples believed that singing attracted Bigfoot. Not just any singing either. Believers hypothesized that singing women could better attract the beast than singing men. Bigfoot, presumably, found women much less threatening. With that theory, I assumed that creatures roaming in the night must be male. Female creatures must not like tunes. It's not evident why I assumed this. Either sex could find females less threatening.

Unless Steve Perry, the lead singer for Journey, belted out a few lines from *Lovin', Touchin', Squeezin'* — then we'd have to fight off scores of salivating Bigfoot Mamas peeking from behind trees ready to mate, probably rubbing their grotesquely ridged nipples against tree bark. Foreplay.

"What *are* you thinking about?" asked my wife.

"Bigfoot females," I said.

Spinner said, "Me too." He grinned.

Christine sighed. "You're wondering how big their tits are." It was a statement, not a question.

"Yes," I said. "No different from your unhealthy fascination with Bigfoot's pecker."

We reached our room and pushed inside. Time to get ready for the second-day meet and greet with the expedition leader and his band of merry travelers.

THE MARTHA EFFECT:
HYPNOTIZED BY BIGFOOT

"Large groups scare wild animals," I said. The man in front of me--I'll call him Leroy-- smiled like a salesman trying to convince someone with a dirt floor to buy a vacuum.

"Large groups attract Bigfoot," said Leroy. He pushed up his ball cap and scratched his forehead. "We'll walk logging trails, speak normal, act normal. That way, we're not threatening. Bigfoot knows his environment. We search for Bigfoot in its own *living room*. Don't you see? Sneaking around won't help us. They'll know we're there."

"How many Bigfoots have you seen?" I asked. "When walking around in a large group?"

(The plural for Bigfoot is Bigfoots, not Bigfeet. I was corrected quickly by the Bigfoot expedition veterans on this point of grammar.)

"We've had multiple sightings. Saw glowing red eyes, too. Heard them following us. Heard whistles and grunts. Even saw something peek out from behind a tree. One threw a rock at me once, hit me on the head. They throw sticks, too."

"Why do they throw sticks and stones?"

"Cuz you're in their territory. They're protecting it."

"Maybe the Bigfoots feel threatened because a *large group*

of people are hiking through their territory, singing, talking, and laughing?"

"Can't be that," said Leroy. "Even if it's one person, they would throw stuff at you."

"Have you ever searched alone?"

"No," said Leroy. "Too scary." He sipped a beer.

"Does anyone search alone?"

"Sometimes Mel does. But none of us go out there without company."

"Then how do you know they throw sticks at people walking at night alone?"

Leroy sipped his beer and smiled at me.

I left Leroy standing by his tent. Around me, expedition participants stuffed backpacks full, replaced batteries in Night Vision Goggles (NVGs), cleaned boot lugs with knives, ate sandwiches, and drank soda or beer. Conversations about other expeditions, sightings, and sounds predominated, most listeners nodding with solemnity when someone spoke of his personal Bigfoot encounter. A member of the expedition leader's command group played sighting DVDs: the Patterson-Gimlin film, followed by the Marble Mountain video, followed by the Snow Walker video, followed by the Paul Freeman video. Newbies like me leafed through photo albums of almost indiscernible blobs identified as possible Bigfoots. Everyone talked of hoaxes, how the Patterson-Gimlin film was surely authentic and *not* a hoax. "Patty" (the female Bigfoot captured on the Patterson-Gimlin film), as she is known in Bigfoot circles, proved without a doubt that a missing link, or additional link, to mankind existed in the Pacific Northwest. Half of the participants thought Bigfoot would be found on this very night. The salmon run was still in full swing, and Bigfoot couldn't resist a nocturnal salmon snack, not here in Olympic National Park.

Not with the true believers singing in the rain.

Just before sunset, groups of Bigfoot searchers drove their SUVs to the rendezvous point near Highway 101, a scooped-out gravel pit bordering high hills and thick underbrush (and, oh by the way, one of the validated sighting areas). Many groups left for pre-scouted destinations. Spinner, Christine, and I hung back, ready for the night but not sure how we wanted to proceed.

While we discussed our options, the EL walked up to us. "There was a sighting last night."

"Where?" I was honestly curious about the who, what, when, where, and how of a Bigfoot sighting.

"On the river."

"Our river?" asked Spinner.

"Yes," said the EL.

"We didn't see anything," I said. "We were the only ones down there."

"Someone saw one on the road."

Christine said, "I was on the road. Nobody said a thing."

"Martha told me what she saw this morning," said the EL. "I thought you should know."

"Who saw something?" asked Christine.

"Martha[1] reported that she saw a Bigfoot entering the river bottom area when the group was on the road." The EL seemed uncomfortable.

"She...saw...a...Bigfoot?" I emphasized each word. Even

---

1   Martha is not her real name.

though I was a non-believer, her after-the-fact report bothered me plenty.

"Yes," said the EL. "She was very frightened at the time. A large bipedal shadow crossed in front of a "no fishing" sign at the end of the road. It disappeared into the woods by the river. She only reported it now because she wanted to ensure that she was confident about what she saw."

"You got to be shitting me," said Spinner. His face began to turn a lovely shade of crimson.

"So Martha saw a Bigfoot walking toward me and Spinner and didn't tell anyone?" I took a deep breath. "She waited until morning?" Maybe it was my voice rising in octaves, or the way my eyes squinted, because suddenly the EL realized why we might, just might, be extraordinarily furious (although, to this day I'm not exactly sure why we were furious).

"I told her she should have mentioned it immediately."

"You think?" Spinner spat out his question and crowded in just behind my shoulder. "I don't think it was Bigfoot. But if it was, we'd have been shit out of luck. Isn't Bigfoot ten times stronger than a man? He could have ripped our limbs off."

"She didn't see a damn thing," said Christine. "She wants attention."

The EL backed away a few steps, as if our anger forced him to retreat.

"What if it was a bear?' I asked.

"I'll talk to her," said the EL.

The EL had tried to appease us. I'm quite sure he empathized.

"She didn't think enough of us to at least warn us over the radio?" asked Spinner.

At that point I almost chuckled, because knowing how the believers felt about Spinner, I could very well imagine one of them withholding critical information for the express purpose of contributing to Spinner's demise. Spinner's brutal and often spot-on observations about Bigfoot sightings, falsification of evidence[2], and financial shenanigans infuriated believers and organizers alike. Bigfoot believers did not like Spinner.

Spinner didn't care about their feelings. He told the truth.

"Why would she wait?" I asked no one in particular.

"Her mind could not make sense of the image," said the EL. "She was in a kind of shock. That happens when people see Bigfoot for the first time."

"Or, she saw how people are treated around here who have a sighting," said Christine. If Christine wasn't such a lady, she might have spit on the EL's boots.

I thought that a likely explanation. Martha was a lawyer, and in my experience, they're often about the attention.

I wondered about her motives on two fronts. First, I wanted to know why she would fake a sighting (if indeed, she had fabricated the sighting). Second, if she believed that she had seen Bigfoot, why wait until the following day to report such a glorious event?

Maybe her sighting happened in this way:

Her mind would not process the image. It was shadow. It was mirage. The radio's crackling static, voices complaining about dead fish stench and loud knocks, the possibility that Bigfoot scooped

---

2   Spinner had been an expert evidence technician for the Michigan State Police.

salmon from the river down there in the dark; surely her imagination dredged the image from her subconscious. Wouldn't the others have noticed? There were several others on the road. She licked her lips. She glanced at the others in the group and then back down the road. Did they see? Did they want to see him?

Ah, but she had a ready explanation for why he blessed only her with his presence. She was standing twenty yards apart from the main group. She was attuned to his existence, his nature. She would not have seen him without his express permission, granted through an extrasensory gift, a fleeting thought that induced her to turn and stare down the road toward a "No Fishing" sign perched on a metal post that stood eight feet tall — that moment when a massive shape completely obscured the sign for a moment, the faint shine of moon and stars providing just the right amount of light so that she would notice him striding purposefully and quietly toward the flopping salmon and the two men down there looking for him. Obviously, anyone who knows Bigfoot realizes that the men by the river are not in danger. Bigfoot is nonviolent.

So, I'll just keep my mouth shut and wait until morning.

Or, it could have gone this way:

What was that? Oh my God! I saw ... something. I don't want to be embarrassed. But it's walking toward the two down by the river ... it's nothing. Right? Oh my God. Was it a bear? My inclination to save myself from embarrassment far surpasses my inclination to warn those two men by the river of any danger.

So, I'll just keep my mouth shut and wait until morning.

Maybe Martha's sighting was a shocking event that happened this way:

She awoke from her dream. In her dream, she was on the road with the others. The men talked of stinking fish and wood knocks over small hand-held radios. So much static. The blonde wife of the one called Denver smirked at the believers ... what a bitch she was. She relived the scene in her dream frame by frame, exactly the same. But in her dream, one frame changed. As she stood apart from the others, she glanced down the long dark road toward the bridge that crossed the river. An instant of moonlight bathed a small area by the "No Fishing" sign with a heavenly glow. There! A shadow of such prodigious size passed by! And it was definitely a male. Oh yes, she could tell even from that distance that Bigfoot's endowment surpassed even the most optimistic estimates.

She had lost time on that road. Like a UFO contactee.

She had seen something and repressed it. It was morning. She would report it.

Or, it happened like this:

I am so jealous that those who claim to have seen Bigfoot are treated like rock stars. I want to be like them. I want to be loved. Last night on the logging road, I thought I saw something, a big- ass shadow by the "No Fishing" sign. I'm almost convinced it was my imagination, or clouds covering the moon, or maybe just my eyes playing tricks on me because it was so very, very dark and I couldn't really make out the sign from that distance anyway. But, hell--it could have been something, right? And I heard wood knocks ... or at least someone heard wood knocks...and the guys along the river thought they smelled Bigfoot. I can sell this! I know I can! I want to be part of the inner circle. Have some fun. Really get to know these wonderful men and women who have seen Bigfoot.

I'll tell the EL that I saw a large shadow that could have been Bigfoot. I'll tell him right after breakfast. And they will like me.

My last guess at how Martha came to see Bigfoot is this:

Bigfoot hesitated in the brush adjacent to the road. He had crossed here many times before. He was accustomed to the "No Fishing" sign, the rushing of the river, and the smell of dead salmon. He was even comfortable with the lights from the far-away dam that provided him with light to navigate through this tricky part of the bottom. But his nose detected a faint, unmistakable human scent. The wind swirled, and even though he was accustomed to the hairless ones' scent, he couldn't comprehend why he could smell them this deep into his hunting time.

Unless they had been here recently … or were here now.

Hunger drove him. He could pass over the road in an instant. Darkness was his friend and he could see very well in the blackness of his forest. Eight feet tall, six hundred pounds, no animal dared challenge him. The human scent faded. Salmon overwhelmed his senses. In a moment of weakness, ignoring his own instincts and evolutionary programming, Bigfoot failed to peek from behind a tree and scan the road both ways. He simply stepped out onto the road with one massive stride. The next stride carried him into the safety of the trees and undergrowth that led to the river bottom. Only a half second from entrance to exit. However, in that instant, a woman caught a glimpse of the last undiscovered ape. Her name was Martha.

The "remembering" of Bigfoot events well after the fact became known as the "Martha Effect."

But the truth is, I have no idea why she waited until morning to report such a cathartic event.

KILLING TIME

True believers are convinced that Bigfoot throws rocks at any human that dares enter its territory. Large Rocks. Small rocks. Boulders. And somehow those rocks always fall just short of the target. Thousands of reported incidents about projectiles lobbed at expedition-goers, and not one skull has been smashed, not one eyeball neatly removed with a well-placed sharp stone.

Not one person's cheek scratched or otherwise harmed.

Spinner and I thought we would run an uncontrolled experiment on the rock-throwing phenomena. We thought it might be an interesting experiment to toss rocks at true believers, to gauge their reactions ... like at the group of hunters that traveled all the way from New York to hunt Bigfoot.

Spinner and I hatched this plan due to the unwavering, courageous nature of these hunters. All of them had experience with hunting large game and frequently spoke in reverential awe about the pet rifles they utilized to remove said game from the valleys and woodlands of our great land.

Comments like:

1. I shot the deer at three hundred yards. Right in the heart.
2. Changing the grain allows me to shoot accurately out to five hundred yards.

3. Best varmint rifle is .223
4. If I saw Bigfoot, I'd shoot it.
5. 300 Winchester Magnum is best for large game.

Their uncompromising bravery made them the perfect test set for our hypothesis.

Mel escorted Spinner and me and the hunters along a trail that side-hilled a rather large mountain. It was early morning, 0100 hours. The stars twinkled bright, the night as still and serene as a placid pond. Unlike the busy Appalachians on the East Coast, the woods kept to themselves here on the Left Coast--noiseless, no deer crunching leaves, no haunting cries of whippoorwills or bobwhites. Eerie. We didn't plan for this windless evening, but the creepy quotient certainly aided our experiment.

One New York hunter said, "This is unnatural quiet. Should be animals moving about."

"Could be something scared them away," said Spinner. "Something big."

"Like a Bigfoot?" I inquired with mock curiosity. "Following us, perhaps?"

I hope I didn't sound too much like Dr. Evil from Austin Powers.

Unaware of our prank, Mel said, "Another guy heard grunting up here last night."

Spinner whispered to me, "Probably a guy taking a dump."

I nodded to him and said out loud, "Might be in Bigfoot territory."

The four New York hunters immediately scooted toward one another, forming an awkward, stumbling circle.

Another hunter, wearing a John Deere hat and a camouflage coat said, "Wish I brought a gun."

It was funny. Them circling the wagons like that.

And Spinner had yet to toss a rock.

Spinner slowed his walk. I caught up to the hunters in front, engaging them in small talk. Mel halted frequently, listening, sniffing, peering into the darkness with Gen-3 night-vision. The hunters hadn't noticed Spinner's disappearance. Only one more important event needed to happen before Spinner started the experiment: We needed Mel to scream for Bigfoot.

The New York hunters were thoroughly convinced, due to the lack of noise and the silent night, that supernatural creatures surrounded us. Saliva dripped from the fangs of male Bigfoots. Red eyes peered at them from behind brush. Juvenile creatures crouched in tree crotches, ready to jump on them like rabid chimps. Evil in hirsute form, bipedal shag-carpet monsters with brains, sharp teeth, and the strength of three grown men. Maybe the hunters felt what women felt when walking alone at night through streets littered with garbage and bums with fetid breath leaning from darkened alleyways to leer at them as they hurried toward safer destinations.

Mel stopped at a bend in the road. A trail split off, wider than an animal trail, presumably made by hikers and campers. But to the New York hunters, this trail was the perfect highway for traveling Bigfoot families, and Bigfoot *constructed* the trail for precisely that purpose. The trail allowed Mel to move deeper into the forest. Being slightly off the road while screaming for Bigfoot was standard operating procedure. Immediately, Mel bent left down the trail and walked in fifty yards. The hunters stopped at the split, peering with great trepidation into the gloom as their Bigfoot tracker disappeared alone into Bigfoot country. Not one hunter followed Mel or offered their considerable protection. Huddling together like scared rabbits with twitching noses, they hunched in expectation of Mel's peculiar howls.

Any moment now.

I stood slightly behind the hunters. Spinner crept along the side of the road, just inside the brush line. Stars twinkled. The moon lay heavy and bloated. Mel waited for the woods to calm, to collect his thoughts before whispering a tribal prayer to the spirits for protection from Bigfoot's magic.

A hunter coughed.

"Shut up," said another hunter. "Mel's gonna do it soon."

Boots scuffled nervously on the stones. I backed away. Slowly. Spinner readied the first stone.

"WAHHHHHOOOOOOOO! WAHHHHHOOOOOOOO! WAHHHHHOOOOOOOO!"

An echoing moan, inhuman to my ears; I jumped even though I had listened to Mel the previous evening. A man sixty-eight inches tall shouldn't be able to produce such earsplitting noise.

Then Mel called again. **"WAHHHHHOOOOOOOO! WAHHHHHOOOOOOOO! WAHHHHHOOOOOOOO!"**

Silence. Utter. Complete. Except for the ringing in my ears. We waited for the elusive return call from a territorial or amorous Bigfoot in close proximity. Most times, coyotes answered Mel. Or owls. Or other people.

Sixty seconds passed.

The New York hunters were convinced that Bigfoot would answer Mel.

The hunters were convinced that Bigfoot existed.

Spinner's throw was so perfectly timed, so delicately planned, so magnificently executed that for an instant I did not know why the hunter closest to the trailhead jumped straight into the air. His horror-stricken high-pitched yelp echoed almost as long as Mel's scream. The other hunters ducked instinctively, closing the circle until they touched, back-to-back-to-back-to-back. Spinner had not aimed for the men specifically, but his first rock struck the hunter squarely in the shoulder.

"Oh my God, oh my God, oh my God..." muttered one hunter.

"Mel, it's throwing stuff at us!" The hunter hit by Spinner's stone boogied in a circle like a disco dancer. "Don't scream no more!"

"We don't have guns. Stupid, stupid, stupid..." chanted another hunter.

The stars still twinkled.

The moon still lay heavy and bloated in the sky.

Spinner threw another rock. It landed squarely in the center of the circle.

They scattered like men getting caught watching porn by their wives. Two of the hunters turned tail and ran past me, back down the road and toward Spinner. Spinner was chucking rocks in rapid fire now, guessing incorrectly that the hunters would figure out that he, and not a barmy Bigfoot, chucked the rocks. Not true. Hunters cowered. Hunters hopped about trying to look everywhere at once. I think a hunter or two pissed their britches.

Then Mel appeared. Mel laughed.

"Come back," I yelled at the running hunters. "There's no Bigfoot!"

43

Realization. Hopping slowed, then stopped. The runners turned around to listen. Another hunter, dulled by the beginning stages of shock, stared at me, uncomprehending. Spinner's last rock landed at my feet, the sharp retort of rock on rock. I bent over and picked up the stone, held it up as proof. In the moonlight they all stared at me. I threw the rock into the woods, over Spinner's head.

"You see," I said. "It's only Spinner."

Spinner emerged from the wood-line, giving his best shit-eating grin. The hunters had not smiled yet, and for a moment I feared a four-on-two ass-kicking.

"That was not cool," said one of the hunters. "I thought we pissed off Bigfoot."

Spinner pointed at me and said, "It was his idea."

"You fuckers," said a hunter.

IN BIGFOOT VERITAS

In vino veritas.

Maybe the new American motto should be *In Budweiser veritas.*

A woman looking for bigfoot after a Budweiser or two; this woman might sound sexy to men, but she's dangerous when she leads other women on a Bigfoot hunt. More dangerous still is that this woman with a Budweiser believes that singing attracts Bigfoot. Not just any songs, mind you, but the lilting tunes of nursery rhymes.

Row, row, row your boat
Gently down the stream,
 Merrily, merrily, merrily, merrily
Life is but a dream.

Other women accept as true these singing theories. Woman with a Budweiser has witnessed Bigfoot no less than three times. Her personal encounters make her a goddess in the Bigfoot community, a Sasquatch princess. Every encounter happened as a direct result of her singing, of her calling out to the lonely creatures that hide behind trees and obscure themselves in brush. From this belief a Bigfoot sub-cult emerged, a sub-cult of true female (and male) believers that sing to Bigfoot as they hike.

Sing.

Or bang pots together.

Or jangle their jingle bells.

Or attempt to talk in loud, non-threatening tones.

This sub-cult thinks that a creature supposedly super-evolved to be secretive, lonesome, camouflaged, and opportunistically omnivorous is curious enough to sacrifice its well-being to listen to bad singing or random human noises; a creature never captured, never killed by truck or auto, never filmed in a proof positive way — the Patterson-Gimlin film notwithstanding — never proven to exist during modern human existence.

Peeking wistfully from behind a tree, a stinking colossal Bigfoot would merrily toe-tap along to warbling idiots tromping through Bigfoot territory, hypnotized by the high-pitched voices of the buzzed females. Is this singing theory any different from that of loggers who believe that the drone of a chainsaw attracts rattlesnakes? Maybe not so different. I have witnessed more rattlesnakes while cutting wood than at any other time in my life. My grandfather swears by the chainsaw/rattlesnake theory; he believes that the chainsaw's "vibration" attracts snakes because "everyone" knows that snakes hunt by *vibration*. When young, I thought it true.

However, is the belief that rattlesnakes are attracted by chainsaws perpetuated by those who cut firewood because *those who cut firewood* are forced to be outside for long periods of time, in usually dense undergrowth, often cutting through downed and rotted logs that harbor snakes? Could the reason that more rattlesnakes are seen while cutting wood be simply because one looks down while wielding a chainsaw, into flora that supports rattlesnake populations? There are many more hypotheses that must be explored before the theory that "I see rattlesnakes only when cutting firewood with a chainsaw, so that means my chainsaw attracts rattlesnakes" can be embraced. The fallacy of the "chainsaw attracting rattlesnakes" argument, if it is false, can be ascribed to the argumentative, often misleading, notion of *post hoc, ergo propter hoc*, Latin for "it happened after, so it was caused by"[3].

So, assuming Bigfoot's existence (there are countless other fallacies attributed to that notion) believers insist that singing attracts Bigfoot more readily than "conventional" clandestine stalk-and-sit hunting techniques. How do the believers know this? Where is the data to back up this notion? Are there documented instances of a solitary man sitting in a camouflage blind who saw Bigfoot only after "singing" searchers joined him and hummed nursery tunes? Is there evidence to support the contrary, where a singing quartet of Bigfoot enthusiasts left a sighting area without spotting Bigfoot, and then shortly thereafter in that same area, a lone searcher utilizing stalking techniques encountered the beast? Do Bigfoot researchers consider that singing, humming, or beating logs with sticks actually arouses the suspicions of heretofore undiscovered animals or "beings"? Maybe the red-eyed visitors are inter-dimensional Goat People or dry-land octopuses or alien

---

3   The logical fallacy is outlined with multiple fallacies in *The Demon-Haunted World* by Carl Sagan. I heartily recommend pages 212–216.

anthropologists or the floating heads of disembodied cavemen ghosts. Maybe Bigfoot is thinking, *I'm getting out of here! Every time that lady sings, those damn goat people run over here! And what's up with those cavemen ghosts? They're so rude!*

So Bigfoot to nursery rhymes is like rattlesnakes to chainsaws—a Miller Analogies Test question for those applying to graduate school.

Bigfoot doesn't throw stones at women invading his territory. Maybe he's looking for some midnight action, and human women provide an easy mark.

Question: Are Bigfoot males the ONLY Bigfoots that roam around at night? Would Bigfoot females be attracted to singing men? Maybe Tom Jones, Gordon Lightfoot, Barry White or John Mayer could entice those randy Squatch ladies. "Dancing in the Moonlight" by King Harvest is my personal number one pick.

REAL TIME PLAYBACK-DEBRIEF

Sap was the artist, the woman who sketched her Bigfoot sightings and expressed interest in Bigfoot's pecker size. Five women and one sixteen-year-old girl follow Sap down a logging road. My wife, Christine, is amongst them, curious about the techniques that Sap uses to find the elusive beast. Christine begins the hike worried.

It's 2200 hours. The sub-cult women had imbibed for well over two hours. Even though they carry no alcohol with them, their nervous tittering and off-key singing mark the beginning stages of inebriation. The sixteen-year-old girl is frightened. Her father, a Bigfoot expedition virgin, had dropped her off with Sap and the female followers just hours before. He left his daughter alone with strangers and then embarked into the dark forest with the man group, led by the EL himself. The poor girl had never been on a Bigfoot expedition, let alone led by someone like Sap. The sixteen-year-old didn't want her father to leave her.

The young girl stood alone. Apart. She crossed her arms over her chest. Christine went to her, befriended her, said, "It'll be alright, honey. Stay close to me."

2215 hours. The girls walk down the trail. Sap leads the group, well in front. All flashlights are turned off, a sliver of moon providing just enough light to navigate the trail. After a few hundred yards, Sap begins to whistle a tune. She hums. She calls for Bigfoot. "Come here, Bigfoot. Here, big boy. Come see us." She sings the first verse of "Row Your Boat."

Clouds drift in front of the moon.

Sap turns and tells everyone to stop. She pulls Gen-2 Night Vision Goggles (NVGs) from her pack and dons them. She walks back to the group.

"I saw red eyes." Sap points down the trail. "With the moon behind the clouds, he'll get brave."

The sixteen-year-old turns to Christine. "Who will get brave?"

Christine whispers, "Bigfoot. They think Bigfoot will get brave."

"Oh my God," whispers the girl. She moves closer, clutching Christine's arm.

"Don't worry." Christine comforts the girl. "They're crazy."

But Christine does worry. Drunken true believers with NVGs...and Sap searching for red eyes and male Bigfoots while singing nursery rhymes.

Oh my God sounds about right.

"Don't you see them?" Sap walks out front, a courageous true believer. "Glowing red eyes. At least two pairs."

A Sap follower pronounces with grave solemnity, "We are not alone."

The sub-cult members inch closer together. Not Sap though. She continues forward into darkness, softly whistling, adjusting her NVGs and calling out to the dancing red eyes of Bigfoots.

Christine and the teenager stand just behind the main group of Sap followers. Christine puts her arm around the teenager's shoulder. The teenager is shaking.

"We won't hurt you." Sap creeps closer to the wood-line. She's almost crouching. "Come out where I can see you. We know you're in there."

Christine peers into the darkness. Squints. The teenager does the same.

"Red eyes," pronounces a follower. "I see them. It's here."

Exciting murmuring from the other true believers, a mumbling rapture, a moment of such undiluted terror and joy that one of the girls begins to choke up. So close to the divine, their hirsute deity creeping about naked on the periphery, a miracle of nature and evolution. Belief wrapped in native legend, decades of searching almost ended by the wisdom and spiritual connection of Sap to Bigfoot. There were only a few like Sap, other Saps, linking with the one true beast. The expedition leader and Sap, both enlightened to the ways of Bigfoot, both united in their goal of finding and cataloging this special, wise and highly evolved biological phenomenon.

Sap speaks to the group. "Act normal. Talk normal. They won't think we're a threat. They like to peek from behind trees. They're shy."

A Sap believer wanders hesitantly away from the main group, passing by Christine and the teenager on her way back down the trail. Christine still stares ahead, where she thinks Sap is looking. The believer keeps walking, stopping approximately ten yards away from Christine. The believer looks for a peeking Bigfoot.

"Something is definitely back there," says the believer. "It's watching us."

"I told you," says Sap. "They're here."

"I see red eyes." The believer's voice quakes. "It's peeking at us."

The teenager sniffles. Christine hugs her tighter. Christine glances backward, then forward. She blinks, straining to make out movement in the shadows.

"Check in the trees, too," commands Sap. "Young ones hide there."

"They're all around us," reports another believer. "They're attracted to us."

A moment of reverential awe. Sap and her believers go silent--contemplative meditation on the greatness of things both large and small. What might come next? Light from heaven? A Bigfoot family unit tromping from the woods with palms outstretched? Such a moment of quiet beauty, a group of humans privileged to be in close contact with these magnificent creatures. A sacred moment for Sap, her singing, her tonal entreaties the missing link in the search for Bigfoot. Because, wasn't "Bigfootese" a tonal language ... like Cantonese?

"I don't see red eyes." Christine squeezes the teenager's shoulder, reassuring the youth.

51

Spell broken, a collective indignant gasp from Sap and her believers.

Sap marches toward Christine and then points into the wood-line. "The red eyes are right there. Don't you see them?"

"I definitely see them," a believer chimes in before Christine answers.

"Nope. Nothing there. No red eyes." Christine stares at Sap, *through* Sap. "Stop scaring the girl."

"Everyone but you sees them," says another believer. Another Sap wanna-be. She taps her foot impatiently.

"I don't see them," says the teenager in a still, soft voice.

"Come with me," says Sap. "I'll show you."

"No," says the girl. "I'm staying with Christine."

"He's here," says Sap.

"No, he's not," says Christine. "You've been drinking."

"I'm not drunk."

"Didn't say you were."

"You just don't want to see."

"That's ridiculous."

Movement in the brush stops the argument. Scurrying. Loud enough to be heard over Christine and Sap. Everyone silent as they wait for whatever monster might appear.

"We're scaring them away." The believer moans in disappointment.

"It's an animal," says Christine. "Opossum probably."

Sap stomps off, toward the spot where she first saw the red eyes. She adjusts her NVGs, scans the trees, looks up into the branches and then down along the ground. Up and down, up and down. "They're gone, Christine. You scared them."

"There was *nothing* there. What's wrong with you people?"

"Let's go back," says a Sapophile. "She ruined it."

END DEBRIEF

We sat around the campfire listening politely to giddy talk of those that heard Bigfoot grunts and saw red eyes. Glowing red eyes. Bemused, Spinner nodded his head at the appropriate times and encouraged those relating their stories to continue educating him on the finer points of Bigfoot-hunting. I listened to Sap's boyfriend try to explain why he mistook the blinking lights of a radio tower for Bigfoot eyes.

You read correctly. This is way too screwed up to be made up.

Sap's boyfriend was a wisp of a man, sporting a light caterpillar mustache and red stringy hair. No taller than five feet seven inches, he weighed about 150 pounds with ten packs of rolled quarters in his pocket. He claimed two legitimate Bigfoot sightings, both of them, while in the company of Sap the singing Sasquatch seducer

I'll call Sap's boyfriend Reggie.

"Red eyes were in the wood line," he said.

"Those were lights," I said. "On a tower."

"I watched the eyes move up the hill. Then I lost the eyes in the darkness and mistook the lights for the eyes."

"Oh my God," I said between bites of Vienna sausage. I love how the Vienna sausages are stuck in that fat infused gelatinous goo. Damn, they're tasty.

"Really," said Reggie. "I know what I'm talking about."

"You're insane," said Spinner.

"Way to make friends," I said to Spinner.

"I've seen Bigfoot," said Reggie. "Twice."

"Want a Vienna sausage?" I held the can out to Spinner. Spinner wrinkled his nose.

"Those things are gross."

"Your loss," I said. I licked my fingers.

"Bigfoot is out there," said Reggie. "You guys just want to make trouble."

I stopped eating my Vienna sausages. Not because Spinner stared at Reggie with violent hatred. No, I stopped sucking the grease off my sausages because Christine stormed into the circle of light like a lioness looking for its young.

"What's up, babe?" I asked.

"Don't leave me with those women again." She stood over me like an avenging goddess, blonde hair spilling from her knit cap, bulky jacket hiding a voluptuous figure. Even Spinner shrunk back from her wrath. Reggie scrunched his frail body deep into his coat.

"Why?" I asked. Innocent.

"They're insane. Drinking. Saying there's red eyes in the trees. Singing to Bigfoot."

"Oh," I said. "Lot of red eyes tonight."

"Reggie saw red eyes," said Spinner. "Blinking red eyes."

Christine turned to him, only now noticing that Sap's boyfriend sat with us. I thought she might apologize to Reggie for calling his girlfriend insane. Maybe she would offer him an olive branch. My wife was a classy broad. She would do the right thing.

"Your girlfriend has lost her mind," said my wife.

Spinner laughed.

Reggie shrunk down into his chair.

I held out my beloved can of Vienna sausages toward Reggie. "Want one?"

MEETING BOB GIMLIN

My wife, Spinner, and I first met Bob Gimlin at the gravel pit/rendezvous point before departing on a mid-afternoon evidence gathering hike. Bob Gimlin is the surviving member of the duo that captured Bigfoot on film October 20th, 1967. Roger Patterson, his partner and the one holding the 16mm camera, died of lymphoma in 1972. In the Bigfoot pantheon, the Patterson/Gimlin film is placed above all other religious texts, eyewitness accounts, hair samples, photos, and similar video captures. The P-G film is regarded as the ultimate proof of Bigfoot's existence by believers.

Bob Gimlin was seventy-four years old when we first met.

The story of the sighting in 1967 and the subsequent filming of Bigfoot has been recounted numerous times in books and other lore. After years of searching, Roger Patterson and Bob Gimlin filmed the creature along Bluff Creek in Northern California. Roger carried a rented Cine-Kodak K-100 and was extremely fortunate to have located and taped Bigfoot on a day where the notoriously nocturnal creature happened to stride in an open patch during good shooting light. Really, Roger's luck couldn't have been better. Bigfoot even posed for him.

At the pit, star-struck fans of Bob (I'll call them FOBs), milled about in a contagious semi-stupor. Spinner, Christine and I must have been infected, because we also shuffled over to Bob's chair. Once again, I was struck by the powerful position that eyewitnesses held in the Bigfoot believer pecking order. Above all the Bigfoot "vetted" eyewitnesses stood Bob Gimlin. Bob held the key to Bigfoot's existence, a grainy 16mm black and white tape that allegedly captures the largest undiscovered ape yet to exist on this planet. FOBs surrounded him, patted his back and fetched his sodas. Some even asked probing questions like:

"Do you believe in Bigfoot?"

"What was it like filming Patty?"

"What was Roger like?"

"Were you scared?

"Was Roger scared?"

To Bob's credit, he answered all their questions with a courtesy I thought truly heroic. For almost forty years, Bob endured these same questions, an endless, mind numbing cacophony. I remembered the EL telling us about Gimlin's joining the group for the expedition, and even then, I imagined his appearance was just another side-show in the Bigfoot carnival tent.

Ladies and gentlemen, step right up. To my left is the amazing Bigfoot tracker. He uses sticks to calculate stride length and can smell the beast from miles away. To my right is the psychic princess of the woods. She can communicate with Bigfoot through an Asian dialect. That's right, folks. Through her, Bigfoot can tell you your future and protect you with his cloak of feel-goody-goodness. Behind me in the main room is Bigfoot's love baby, a hairy creation frozen in ice, half-human and half-beast. Folks, I've seen its mama and let me tell you, she's no looker!

Last and certainly not least, we have the man who came face to face with Bigfoot and lived to tell about it. He's here. You can speak with him and ask him what it was like to have Bigfoot in his gun sights. For only five dollars, you can spend ten minutes with the man we all know as Bob Gimlin!

If this was a sideshow, he handled the marks with aplomb. His easy way with people created an authentic experience. Either Bob had practiced this effortless back-and-forth for years, or Bob was the genuine article. I'm inclined to believe the latter.

"Hello," I said after most of the FOBs had departed. I introduced myself. I introduced my wife. Bob and I shook hands.

"Hello, lovely lady," said Bob to my wife. He tipped his cowboy hat. Bob's entirely pleasant baritone voice made me like him immediately. If a voice matched body type, Bob should have sounded like Dudley Moore.

Spinner introduced himself. Bob nodded kindly. I wondered if one of the believers had warned Bob about Spinner.

"Having fun?" I asked.

"Yes," he said. "I am."

"Mind if I sit here beside you?" asked my wife. Folding chairs had been left by the FOBs.

"Not at all. Never turn down a pretty lady."

I didn't feel threatened by Bob's charm. I thought I could take him if he tried to go Bigfoot with my wife.

After a moment of not too uncomfortable silence my wife asked, "What do you do for a living?"

"I train horses," answered Bob. "Have a little piece in Washington. Got some animals up there."

"I love horses," said my wife. "I always wanted to ride."

And with that statement, Bob Gimlin and my wife talked for almost an hour on the virtues of horse riding and training. Spinner and I listened. I noticed that Bob's demeanor changed; he perked up considerably. He laughed. He gesticulated. He explained the minutiae of horse breaking and secrets he used to win horses over. As the sun sank lower, only the four of us were left at the gravel pit. Spinner and I eventually drifted away, leaving Bob and Christine to their conversation. We never mentioned Bigfoot to Bob, and I know Bob appreciated that deeply. He told me so four years later during an interview with him in his home state.

HUMPING
THE HARMONIC UNIVERSE

Mothman and Bigfoot are related. Not like a brother and sister, or cousins. That would be weird. Mothman and Bigfoot are related by the one single fact that wouldn't be obvious to someone like me, a non-believer, a doubting Thomas. You see, Mothman and Bigfoot are truly alive and kicking, playing hopscotch and Red Rover on a playground with green aliens somewhere in Area 51. These creatures are hidden from the public's view by the Men in Black, the MIB--government operatives who dress in black suits and wear dark sunglasses.

Operatives like me.

Conspiracies are true. Right? Must be! John F. Kennedy was killed by the mob, CIA, or both. Neil Armstrong never walked on the moon; he hopped about on top of manufactured lunar dust inside a top-secret movie studio. Our own government orchestrated the 9/11 attacks (because, as you know, fire can't melt steel and President Bush was a globalist). Roosevelt knew well in advance that the Japanese would attack Pearl Harbor. Hell, Roosevelt planned it! In Roswell, extraterrestrial biological entities crash landed. It's only a matter of time before the evil Grays take over our beloved earth.

And behind this intrigue are top government officials

manipulating our present and future like omnipresent marionette masters. Those strings stapled to our reality represent the MIB.

Government operatives.

People like me.

At least, that's what the Bigfoot searchers thought. They knew that I was once an Air Force intelligence officer and now worked in the National Security Agency as a Department of Defense contractor. My presence validated their deepest fears and, perversely, their most fervent hopes. That final night of the Washington State expedition, I received the requisite sideways glances, the furtive maneuverings, the whispered doubts as to my truthfulness. Only a matter of time before the question would bubble up. A stumble-bum would saunter up casually, beer in one hand, cigarette in another. He would begin with small talk, eventually sliding up close to me in preparation for the ultimate inquiries.

"Where is Bigfoot hidden? Are you here to write our names down? To make a list of crazy Bigfoot people? Are you here to discredit us? NSA knows that Bigfoot is real, doesn't it? You spooks are all the same. Mind-screwing America with your conspiracies and phone taps and dossiers. We know why you're here. Bigfoot is real! The government doesn't want us to know about him. About the missing link. You're a spy for them. We're a threat, because we know! The truth is out there!"

Then the stumble-bum would belch and pick his nose absentmindedly while staring at me with haughty contempt.

The Bigfoot believers had a point. Why else would I join their group in the woods, wandering around hooting and hollering for Bigfoot? I worked in NSA, for God's sake. The government, despite our inability to fix healthcare, destroy Al-Qaeda or balance the budget, could somehow hide an eight-foot bipedal monster inside a massive Frigidaire outside of Las Vegas.

Makes perfect sense.

Maybe some of these conspiracies are true. Possible. Not probable. But possible. Odd occurrences do happen every so often in and around the United States government. The very fact that I am writing this could be an awkward attempt to convince the reader that Bigfoot couldn't exist, that belief in Bigfoot is preposterous. Hell, the government could have chartered me to write this book as an experiment in deception and disinformation.

Because I'm a government operative.

Because I roast marshmallows with perfect precision. Instead of charcoal black, my marshmallow always comes out of the fire toasty brown. Only a highly trained agent can roast a marshmallow like that.

Coincidentally, I was alone roasting a marshmallow when someone did saunter up to me and asked, "Tell me about Fort Lewis."

Please no.

"I know you government types have secret documents on what those soldiers saw in Fort Lewis."

I sighed. Three days and two nights of discussing the inane with true believers had tested my patience. But my façade of kindness served me well. Christine and Spinner had ribbed me nonstop for my sincerity, a propensity for over-the-top kindness and my innate ability to connect with every true believer. True believers took me at my word. Because of my talents, I was able to get many of these individuals to share private observations and deeply felt beliefs.

Maybe I was an unbelieving, ignorant shit-for-brains who just couldn't grasp the big picture.

I grew weary of the charade.

But, as always, I was curious, so I smiled and patted the empty camp chair next to me. "Sit down," my smile told him. "Tell me what you think."

It had been fun at first. The smell of dead fish, excited jabbering on two-way radios, the stories, the red eye sightings, the dripping sarcasm, arguments between Bigfoot theorists, the observations of sexual want and tension — it all made for a stimulating trip. But unlike the believers, Spinner, Christine, and I were pretending. Pretending gets you only so far. True believers never grow weary of discussing Bigfoot scatological finds, mating habits, food sources, migration paths, DNA samples, the Patterson-Gimlin film, competing Bigfoot groups, eyewitness accounts, glowing red eyes, stick shelters, Gigantopithecus Blacki, Homo Erectus, the veracity of video evidence, sleep paralysis, and other cryptic hypotheticals.

Or government conspiracies.

Military bases are where most government conspiracies start, right? Roswell is near Nellis Air Force Base and Area 51. UFOs were spotted in England, right outside of the NATO air base RAF Bentwaters. Pearl Harbor is a naval base. It is no accident that Fort Lewis in Washington State is the epicenter of the Bigfoot government cover-up.

Is there an Area 51 for Bigfoots? Does a high, electrified fence surround a government-funded "zoo" where experiments are conducted on Bigfoot families? Does a top-secret special operations team capture Bigfoots? Is Halliburton involved? How many Bigfoots have been captured? Does the Forest Service kill Bigfoots to prevent categorizing Bigfoot as an endangered species? Are Bigfoot skeletons stashed in the Smithsonian? Are government documents that mention Bigfoot stored for safekeeping? Are Bigfoot witnesses killed? Are Bigfoot witnesses discredited by the government, made to look insane through planted newspaper articles and university scientists?

The man sat down next to me. I'll call him Frank.

"The only stuff I know about Fort Lewis is from what I've read on the internet." I shrugged. "In 1978 an Army grunt on Fort Lewis supposedly shot a Bigfoot in the chest."

Frank gave me an unconvinced eyebrow raise. "You know about it because you see secret documents."

Ridiculous. People like Frank, who have never worked with classified material, are the only assholes to make such pronouncements. There are hundreds of thousands of cleared individuals: cleared meaning those with access to classified information. However, not only does each service and agency protect their own documents through password protection, Public Key Infrastructure, and caveats, there are multiple classification levels (Confidential, Secret, Top Secret, Sensitive Compartment Information or SCI, special access programs, etc.) and even those cleared through their respective agencies must have a "need-to-know" to access documents in another agency. This need-to-know is how classifications and secret programs are kept "compartmented."

Compartmentalizing programs makes it easy to control who knows what about what, allowing security officers to manage distribution of classified information. Obviously, someone cleared *Secret* cannot view *Top Secret* documents. And those cleared *Top Secret* cannot view *SCI* material. Within each clearance level are multitudes of Special Access Programs (SAP). These SAPs are labeled by digraphs (a two-letter identifier) or trigraphs (a three-letter identifier) that require special permissions to access. Only a select few can access each digraph or trigraph within each classification level within each agency. To make matters more confusing, hundreds to thousands of SAPs are imbedded inside different intelligence disciplines: Human Intelligence (HUMINT), Electronics Intelligence (ELINT), Communications Intelligence (COMINT), Foreign Instrumentation Signals Intelligence (FISINT), Imagery Intelligence (IMINT), Measurement and Signature Intelligence (MASINT), Open Source Intelligence (OSINT), Acoustic Intelligence (ACOUSTINT) and Geospatial Intelligence (GEOINT).

But that's not all.

Due to US Code law and policy, foreign and domestic intelligence collection and dissemination are partitioned. FBI, ATF, US marshals, Homeland Security, state and local agencies are the main collectors and users of domestic intelligence. NSA, CIA, DIA, military services and other agencies comprise those that collect and disseminate foreign intelligence. Only in cases of special dispensation can intelligence be shared across domestic and foreign intelligence agencies. Code law and policy that direct the separation of foreign and domestic intelligence agencies is predicated on Executive Order 12333. Read it.

But that's not all

Analysts create their own documents based on sources

and intelligence. Many of these documents are "Originator Controlled" (ORCON), which means they cannot be released without the permission of the "originator," the document author. ORCON documents are prevalent in each discipline, under each SAP, under each digraph or trigraph, within each agency, within each office in every agency and based on either domestic or foreign intelligence. It is not even possible to count the number of ORCON documents that cannot be disseminated, and for the most part, will never be disseminated, outside the intelligence discipline, clearance level, and SAP.

But that's not all.

Combine the above menagerie of disciplines, special programs, and intelligence bifurcations with the decades and decades of intelligence-gathering, and you have trillions of bytes of information stored digitally and billions of hard-copy documents hidden in vaults across the country and even throughout the world. It is impossible for an intelligence analyst working in a government agency or military service to know what's happening in the other agencies and services due to the compartments, SAPs, intelligence disciplines, and US code law that must be followed. It is impossible for an analyst to read all intelligence documents (digital and hard copy), to peruse all intelligence briefs ever made, to just leisurely study the entire classified history of the United States, both foreign and domestic — and while taking the time to study said documentation stumble upon a sensitive Bigfoot government program.

For the love of God.

Even if there were a classified Bigfoot program, I would not be privy to it, unless I was specifically in the know as a read-in member of that caveat. And *never* would I stumble upon documentation that mentions a classified Bigfoot program.

Well, the word *never* is an absolute, which intelligence analysts aren't supposed to use. I should say *almost* never.

Never say never.

There might be a new discipline: *Analytical Sasquatch Studies Intelligence*.

ASSINT.

I do not have access to ASSINT. I am not ASSINT cleared. I have never read a document marked TOP SECRET//ASSINT.

But Frank believed ASSINT existed.

He waited for me to respond to his statement about me reading secret Bigfoot documents.

I said, "I have not read any secret Bigfoot stuff--and if I did, I couldn't tell you anyway."

"I knew it," said Frank.

"What do you know?" I asked

"There's a secret government program."

"How do you know this?" I asked.

"You just told me without telling me," said Frank.

"How do you figure that?"

"You can't tell me if you know, so you told me you didn't know but said it in such a way as to make me think there is a secret Bigfoot group." He said this with such smug satisfaction that I almost laughed out loud.

I shook my head. I roasted my marshmallow. "We shouldn't be talking about this," I said.

Shocked and spiritually fulfilled silence followed from Frank. As far as Frank was concerned, I had given him the unadulterated source confirmation that a government agency studied Bigfoot, and probably had a stuffed Bigfoot standing in the lobby of an underground facility in Nevada.

"I understand," said Frank.

I reached over and shook his hand.

"So tell me about Fort Lewis," said Frank.

I sighed.

Mentioning that I worked as a DoD contractor, in the NSA no less, would come back to haunt me.

INSANITY ENVY

Coyote howls excited the Bigfoot believers, because coyote howls might actually be Bigfoots emulating coyotes for the express purpose of confusing those humans looking for specific Bigfoot howls.

That's right.

Whether it be whistling or talking in "Samurai," Bigfoot is a highly capable mimic, able to "ape" sounds that other animals, like humans, make. Their ability to mimic is one of those many highly adapted qualities that allows them to exist on the periphery, never captured, never found dead, always a step ahead of those hairless beings that constantly tromp about in forests.

And on this night, the coyote I heard could theoretically be a Bigfoot talking in Coyote speak to warn his Bigfoot brethren that we were there, watching, waiting with Gen-3 night-vision and cameras.

I sat against a rock at the side of a fast-moving river, dressed in full camo, scanning the opposite bank for any sign of movement. Nothing so far, nothing for hours. I suspected that we might spy a bear eventually, or one of those coyotes that could be Bigfoot. Washington State in and around Olympic National Forest is a breathtaking treasure of massive trees combined with rainforest flora and fauna. Elk, deer, otters, and bear are as exotic and exciting as any mythical creature. We hadn't seen much in the way of animals, since most Bigfoot-searching happened at night. I closed my eyes, listened to the river as it heaved and bubbled around boulders. The rocks protected me from the breeze, but a chilly draft brushed against my face every so often. I repositioned my backside, putting more of my weight on the left buttock. Mist sometimes rained down, maybe a combination of blown river water and rain from the fast-moving clouds overhead. There were clouds darker than the night sky but allowing for stars to peek through now and then. No one else in the group talked, the silence of the last evening's search a tell-tale sign that the excitement for the hunt waned; another expedition with no specimen. But to hear the believers chatter away, this expedition had resulted in multiple sightings and auditory events. Stick shelters had been found. Indefinable grunts and mimic sounds indicated Bigfoot activity. A few expedition- goers reported odd psychic ailments, like goosebumps, hairs standing up on their arms and head, feelings of dread, feelings of nausea, and hysterical fear.

One man reported that a large stone struck him in the back, obviously tossed from a thicket across the river and half way up a mountain. Only Bigfoot had that kind of major-league arm: Roger Clemens on HGH, anabolic steroids, and injected adrenaline.

I thought of the hunters Spinner and I had duped. I smiled.

Spinner sat beside me. He had been quiet most of the evening. I nudged him.

"What's up, dude?" I whispered to him. "How's it hanging?"

He shrugged, and then asked, "Want to hear a story?"

"Sure," I said. I was so bored. Spinner's stories about his experiences on the job with the Michigan State Police usually cracked me up or horrified me, or both. What better way to pass the time?

Spinner began:

I was dispatched to a traffic crash. I think it was in 2003 or so. It was a cool night, not quite winter, but maybe late October from what I remember of the weather. I arrive at the scene and there is this white Pontiac 6000 LE (luxury edition) with chrome rims, headlight covers, chrome wiper blades – basically pimped out – sitting off the road smashed; one of those older cars that's really nothing but a piece of crap covered in chrome. I can't really recall the other vehicle involved in the crash--a sport utility, I think--but the occupants were standing huddled in a circle, talking. Sitting on the shoulder of the road near the Pontiac, a twenty-something male held his head in his hands and mumbled to himself.

I rushed over to a young male, assuming that he must be injured in some way. I asked him, "Are you okay?"

"Yeah," he replied, "but my goolie is all fucked up."

I searched the memory banks of my brain trying to define "goolie," but came up dry. I thought I must have him wrong, so I said, "Where are you hurt?"

"It's just my goolie, it's all fucked up."

I had heard him correctly. I had absolutely no idea what a "goolie" was. I was an un-hip, middle-aged cop. I'm not always (okay, never) at the cutting edge of the current lingo. I figured that goolie must have something to do with his head or neck. I didn't see any blood but still thought I should find out about his hurt goolie, so

I could translate for those medical personnel driving the ambulance that I could hear approaching. I asked, "What exactly is a goolie? I don't get it."

Obviously irate with me he said, "You lookin' at it now, man, can't you see my goolie's lying in the ditch. Damn, you're dumb."
For a brief second, I panicked, thinking perhaps a part of this young man's body was lying in the ditch. I did a quick visual survey and confirmed that all his appendages appeared intact. I became irritated and said, "You are going to have to try to explain because I don't understand what the fuck you are trying to say. What the hell is a goolie?"

The young gentleman jumps to his feet (obviously pissed off), storms over to his Pontiac and says in a loud voice while pointing at each digit on the 6000LE letters on vehicle's trunk lid, "G, O, O, O, L, E – goolie! What the fuck don't you get!"

I started laughing. Not a chuckle, mind you, but a whole body-encompassing shake. Spinner's story, told with an almost monotone lilt of fact and peculiar struck me as the single most hilarious tale ever told. Sleep deprivation was a factor in my hysteria, but as I guffawed and rolled on the rocks, Spinner started laughing with the same out-of-control wheezing and flapping of arms. I couldn't stop but could only mumble GOOLIE over and over.

"GOOLIE!" cried Spinner.

Our expedition brethren stared us with a mixture of amusement and fury.

"You're going to scare Bigfoot," whispered Reggie. "Shut up!"

If I had been laughing hard before, nothing could

compare to the frenzy of uncontrolled wailing that erupted from my mouth, a soul-shaking howling that freed the pent-up ridiculousness that had been chasing me all expedition. Men dressed in full camouflage, holding Gen-3-night vision cameras, staring at Spinner and me as if *WE* were the crazy ones. Men scanning river banks for a creature as likely to exist as an ogre, men spending money and time to search for truth wrapped in hairy skin! And, now, the *GOOLIE* story would be the act that scared Bigfoot away, the laughter of sleep-deprived men who could no longer rationalize the world's largest snipe hunt.

Oh my dear Lord, did I laugh.

I cried.

Spinner leaned against me, losing strength as he sobbed on my shoulder.

"*GOOLIE,*" I repeated through sniffles.

And we wailed again. The men scooted away from us, mumbling under their breaths, no doubt furious at our lack of respect.

Furious at our sacrilege.

Mel giggled some, but he too thought we showed serious disrespect to the other expedition goers.

"I'm going to separate you two if you can't be quiet," he whispered through clenched teeth.

OF ALL THE BIGFOOTS,
WHICH BIGFOOT IS TRUE?

I saw someone I knew from the Washington State Bigfoot expedition on a new Travel Channel show about those who search for Bigfoot. This "someone" is a Bigfoot expert (I am still not sure how anyone can be an *expert* on a mythological creature). This someone theorized that females attract Bigfoot far more readily than males, and that singing songs attracts the beast. Nursery rhymes mostly, because nursery rhymes are easy to remember.

Exactly what I had been told. *Post hoc, ergo propter hoc.*

Stunned, I watched this program, watched as the narrator spoke in heavy tones, watched as the camera panned through a darkened forest. At any moment, Bigfoot could emerge from the trees, stalking its prey, ears wiggling to the sounds of off-key singing or humming. At least, that's what they wanted the viewer to believe.

Didn't happen.

Never happens.

Of all the Bigfoot television programs dedicated to those searching for the beast, there has never been a sighting, never been a real print discovered, never been anything that proves Bigfoot exists. Most of these Bigfoot programs rely on shaky eyewitness sightings and eerie background music, because nothing else exists to document. Usually, a man with a flannel shirt, a touch of throat cancer from chewing tobacco and a missing front tooth gesticulates as he tells of his "encounter." Most eyewitness accounts go something like this:

Interviewer: What did you see on March 10th, last year, Mr. Butz?

Butz: Can't explain it really. Saw a large black thing squatting in the middle of my neighbor's sod field. I stopped my truck, cuz I never seen nothing like that. Looked like a big stump.

Interviewer: Was it a stump?

Butz: Nope. (Butz spits tobacco juice to the side.) I smelled an awful smell. Like a cow fart. Wind was coming across the field. Must've come from that black thing. And I ain't never saw a stump there before.

Interview: Had cows been in the field?

Butz: Not that day. Weird, huh?

Interviewer: Yes, Mr. Butz. (Announcer speaks slowly, voice reflecting great tension and curiosity.)Very intriguing.

Butz: So, I stop and watch it. I feel like it's watching me.

Interviewer: Did it move?

Butz: I think it did, but the wind was blowing, like I said. (Butz spits again.) I got the goosebumps, because I thought

I saw hair blow off of it.

Interviewer: You must have great eyesight.

Butz: Nods. Surely do. Got glasses last year for the first time and I'm pushing fifty.

Interview: How long did you watch?

Butz: At least a minute or two. But it held still. Bigfoots do that, I hear. Camouflage themselves to look like their environs. This one acted like a stump.

Interviewer: Did you have binoculars with you?

Butz: In the glove compartment I had me a brand-new pair. But I never thought to get them out. Maybe Bigfoot was using its psychic blocking ability to stop me from thinking about those binos in the glove compartment. Someone from the Bigfoot Searchers Group who interviewed me about this last week told me that the Bigfoots are psychic.

Interviewer: So, you saw something that looked like a large black stump in a field. This stump was obviously Bigfoot camouflaging itself as a stump. You knew it was a Bigfoot because it smelled like cow farts and you had never noticed a stump in that part of your neighbor's field before. You forgot about your new binoculars, so you deduce that the camouflaged Bigfoot must have been using its highly evolved psychic abilities to prevent you from remembering your binoculars. Plus, you saw hair blowing off the stump during a windy day. Is this correct?

Butz: Sounds right.

Interviewer: Wouldn't the Bigfoot use its psychic ability to block its odor?

Butz: (Laughs.) Nothing could block that smell.

Interviewer: And you left after a couple of minutes?

Butz: Yep. (Spits tobacco.)

Interviewer: Why didn't you walk across the field? Get a closer look?

Butz: That's plum crazy.

Interviewer: Had you been drinking?

Butz: Only a couple beers. (Butz becomes indignant.) Hell, it was in the afternoon!

Interviewer: Did you go back? See if the stump was there?

Butz: I sure did. And, I saw a stump close to where I saw the Bigfoot, but it was a much smaller stump. Like I said, it was CAMOUFLAGED.

Interviewer: Thank you Mr. Butz. (Interviewer turns toward the camera and speaks to his audience.) You've just heard an amazing account of a Bigfoot sighting here in Oklahoma. Seymour Butz was simply minding his own business when he witnessed a Bigfoot sitting in the middle of his neighbor's field, camouflaged as a stump. After being attacked by psychic energy and an overpowering odor, Seymour fled the scene. All of us must ask ourselves if, indeed, Bigfoot exists.

Like the fictional Mr. Butz, many of those that Spinner,

Christine, and I talked with during our expedition believed that Bigfoot used psychic ability, camouflage, and smell to hide from humans. Native Americans, especially, believe that Bigfoot is a magic creature able to hex anyone and steal the soul of any human that dares stare into its eyes. Stories told beside campfires perpetuate these belief systems among Native Americans and ordinary Bigfoot-believing- Americans alike.

Makes for a hell of a horror movie. I'll write a screenplay called *Soul-Stealing Sasquatches.* As much as I respect our native cultures, and as much as I like Mel, I cannot wrap my arms around a theory that a Bigfoot can take a soul with their eyes. Stories about soul-stealing Sasquatches, told to Bigfoot true believers, validates their belief.

A colleague of mine from my work place believes in Bigfoot. He explained that Bigfoot is a traveler from another energy plane that protects and watches over us ignorant human life forms. Because, as most other creatures that reside in the harmonic universes (HU) above us know, humans are the dumbest and the most fortunate of the species to reside in HU 1 through HU 5. I humored my colleague and listened to his beliefs on mystical beings, telepathic communication, and Keylontic science. He placed his hand on my shoulder and said, "Bigfoot is a guardian of the human race. Bigfoot visits me in dreams."

I did not find this particularly believable, but I also did not condemn him for his credence in what he referred to as the *Guardian Alliance*[4]. He handed me a book called *Voyagers, The Sleeping Abductees* by Ashayana Deane. In the book, the true

---

4   As noted in *Voyagers,* the Guardian Alliance (GA) is a cooperative organization through which an enormous variety of different interstellar, multi-dimensional and inter-time species and races work together to assist in the evolution of developing cultures throughout the multidimensional universe. They are at odds with the Intruders mentioned on the following page.

name of Bigfoot is revealed: Queventelliur. Queventelliurs are described as large, long-haired apelike beings of great intelligence and sensitivity, which are occasionally glimpsed on earth as they monitor Earth's environment for guardian purposes.

My colleague warned me that the book was very advanced, and it was okay if I did not comprehend the entirety of its message. The author writes that her "implications are so intrinsically profound that at times it seems unbelievable."

Following are excerpts from her book:

"In 1969, at four years of age, I had my first conscious initiation into the contemporary world of extraordinary events, as I was physically abducted from my driveway in broad daylight by a small grey being with large black eyes ... I endured three years of ritual abductions in which I was physically taken from my bed at night and transported to a silent spacecraft, escorted by a trio of identical gray beings.

*"Collectively I refer to the legions of the Zeta-Dracos alliance and any other Visitors from elsewhere who hold agendas that are detrimental to the evolution of humans as the **Intruders**.*

*"The information contained within the Voyagers Series Books, Kathara Bio-Spiritual Healing System, Tangible Structure of the Soul Accelerated Bio-Spiritual Evolution Program, and related materials produced through the 3 legitimate Guardian Alliance (GA) Speakers, represents translation of ancient records. These ancient records exist in physical form as a set of 12 Silver-metallic discs called the Cloister-Dora-Teura-Plate Libraries or **CDT** Plates. The 12 CDT-Plates are holographic recording, storage and transmission devices that hold massive amounts of data in encrypted, electromagnetic, scalar-standing-wave form...*

"The CDT plates were manufactured by the Taran Priests of Ur and Maharaji Sirian Blue Human 'Holy Grail Line' races of the Council of Azurline, often collectively called the Azurite or Eieyani Races, on Density-2 Sirius B, GA Signet Council-6 and guardians of D-6 Sirius B Star Gate-6 in the Universal Templar Complex. In 246,000 BC, CDT-Plates were presented as a gift to the Urtite Human Race, the Seed Race of the contemporary human lineage ...

Amazing. Ashayana Deane might

1. Be an inspired modern prophet
2. Possess the greatest imagination of our time
3. Be insane
4. Have been abducted by aliens
5. Have found a money-making niche as well as being one hell of a fiction writer

My opinion, based solely on my experience with the Guardian Alliance and black-eyed intruder aliens, is that this belief system is poppycock, cobbled together through reading science fiction books, studying fringe cults, fighting suppressed childhood psychoses and then filling in logic gaps with secretive "CDT" plates and a promise of more knowledge and affirmation "in the future." It's the perfect recipe to attract marginalized people that live outside societal norms, who are desperately searching for an identity, a unique and special dispensation that puts them either above or apart from an ignorant and myopic populace (like me). It's a rather perverse narcissism, where one's relationship with alien anal probes and twelve-strand DNA beings cultivates universal enlightenment. Anyone can believe anything. It's what makes America great.

Sasquatch, Bigfoot, Oh-Mah, and Stick People now have another name: Queventelliur. Queventelliur is the ultimate environmentalist, bridging dimensions for the betterment of mankind. He is energy. He is a member of the Guardian Alliance. He cannot be killed, cannot be captured. Conveniently, his existence cannot be proven, because of his energy-being status. If an energy being cannot be killed and stuffed (like a big trophy buck), how in the hell can someone like me prove that Bigfoot cum Queventelliur is out there?

What is Bigfoot? Is Bigfoot a missing link, a Gigantopithecus Blacki that survived like the Coelacanth? Is Bigfoot a "magic man," a creature that can take a person's soul? Is Bigfoot a card-carrying member of the Guardian Alliance, an inter-dimensional environmentalist who sometimes donates to the Sierra Club? Or is Bigfoot something entirely different?

ORGIES AT THE FEET OF THE GODS

Spinner, Christine, and I were invited to a Bigfoot party on the final night of the expedition, right around the time that Mel finished a bizarre and frightening story about a hunter's son following a psychic and ill-intended Bigfoot into the woods. We politely declined the invitation. We had heard through the grapevine that Bigfoot groupie women enjoyed imbibing beer and wine heavily during these parties. And rumors of persistent flirting and "hooking up" between expedition-goers prevented us from attending. During the expedition, I could not help but notice that a select few of the females valued their quality time in the presence of the almighty expedition leader. The EL's pronouncements about the nature and proclivities of Bigfoot were hailed as gospel, an unalterable truth that could not be denied, could not be ignored, could not be forgotten. Bigfoot believers listened with sparkling eyes and slightly opened mouths as the EL and his inner circle discussed mating habits, food sources, migration patterns and shelter building. Conversations about these topics were convoluted yet authoritative … almost like a presidential debate.

Bigfoot Believer #1 (BB1): I saw two young trees with their tops bent sideways. Weird.

EL: How far apart were the trees?

BB1: About twenty yards.

EL: Congratulations! You just found highway markers for traveling Bigfoots. They are close by … maybe watching us now.

Bigfoot Believer #2 (BB2): I'm getting goosebumps. Like something is watching me. The Bigfoots sense we are talking about them. I can feel it in my bones!

BB1: This is so exciting. I found a Bigfoot road!

EL: The snapped tops are also warnings to other Bigfoots and humans, territorial markers.

Spinner: Maybe the wind snapped them.

EL: Two trees twenty yards apart? Snapped at approximately the same height? (EL laughs derisively.) I don't think so.

Spinner: He never said they were snapped at the same height.

BB1: But they were snapped at the same height! I remember now! I smelled something funny too. Like a wet dog.

EL: Bigfoot might emit a giant skunk smell, to ward off enemies.

Spinner: This is insane.

Obviously, Spinner and the EL did not get along. The EL recognized Spinner for what Spinner was: a man who called things as he saw them. Spinner believed that the EL was a shyster, fleecing true believers by conducting paid expeditions in public parks. As for me, I can never say for sure what's in a man's heart. It's possible that the EL believed with mind and soul that Bigfoot existed. Or, he could have recognized that true believers could be fooled into paying outrageous money to "hook up" with fellow believers in a paid quest to find, or at least hear, Bigfoot. Extra money could also be made by advertising said expedition as "adventure camping" and charging those with means an exorbitant fee for a lark in the woods. Either way, it seemed good business, with the more than twenty expedition-goers tromping about in the woods, whistling and hooting for giant snipe. Even with discounted group rates, the EL most likely pulled in 20K or more. Hell, I paid him a few thousand clams myself. Not a bad take for a weekend.

I confess. I wanted to believe in that remote possibility that "something was out there." What a grand fantasy! In the woods, a race of super hairy giants tromped about, using whistles and grunts for communication, foraging for nuts and berries — living, breathing natural wonders untouched by the dirty hands of man. Shy and inquisitive, they existed in harmony with earth, unconcerned with interacting on any scale with the hairless beasts who invaded their forests. Is it probable that creatures such as these exist? Of course not. But maybe, just maybe, I thought it *possible*.

Hadn't someone captured a coelacanth, thought to be extinct for tens of millions of years? In 1938, Marjorie Courtenay Latimer discovered the coelacanth in a fisherman's catch. What a discovery! Since that time, "the extinct" coelacanth has been hooked a few times. The latest catch was reported in the *National Geographic News*:

May 22, 2007 — Though he may have only been angling for dinner, the Indonesian fisher who caught a rare coelacanth has instead snagged a barrage of worldwide media attention.

Yustinus Lahama captured the fish — which scientists not long ago believed had gone extinct with the dinosaurs — Saturday near Bunaken National Marine Park, off Sulawesi Island.

The four-foot (1.2-meter), 110-pound (50-kilogram) specimen lived for 17 hours in a quarantine pool, an "extraordinary" feat considering the cold, deep-sea habitat of the fish, marine biologist Lucky Lumingas of the local Sam Ratulangi University told the Associated Press. Lumingas plans to study the carcass.

Scientists were shocked when a coelacanth (pronounced SEE-la-kanth) was found off Africa's coast in 1938. They had believed the fish went extinct 65 million years ago, as did a related lineage of prehistoric fishes.

The fish has been a source of fascination ever since. Several other coelacanths have been caught in recent decades, including another in the species-rich waters of Sulawesi in 1998.

Coelacanths usually reach five feet (1.5 meters) in length, have limb-like fins, and are covered in hard scales and toothy outgrowths that protect their bodies from rocks and predators.

Unlike other fish, they also give birth to live young.

Imagine that! Having a good old time, drinking beer, swapping stories with your pal about glory days, admiring your cooler full of crappie, and suddenly, your pole bends double and you hook a prehistoric creature that gives birth to live young.

Maybe the Loch Ness monster exists.

Or Champ in Lake Champlain.

Or Dog People.

Or chupacabra.

Or the unicorn.

How about a centaur?

A minotaur?

How about the Scylla and Charybdis?

What about Mothman?

Is Bigfoot simply the land-based version of the coelacanth?

Fossils. We need fossils. The difference between the coelacanth and the centaur is striking. There are no fossil records of a centaur. For that matter, unless you believe insane ramblings on the internet, there have been no unicorn horns discovered. I have not yet heard about an amazing unearthing of a Charybdis jawbone. Where are the remains of a blood-sucking chupacabra?

Excitement is to find something that once was or something that never existed. New species of plants and animals are discovered every day. I wish Bigfoot existed. Photo evidence is spotty; the Patterson-Gimlin film is most likely a fraud (in my own estimation) and eyewitness accounts are tainted by insanity or fiction or made innocently by those mistaking Bigfoot for a known animal.

There are no bones, Gigantopithecus Blacki notwithstanding.

An ocean is so much larger by volume, undiscovered in its core, able to hide species and mysteries much more effectively than a national park outside Seattle, Washington. An Aqua-Bigfoot — hirsute version of Kevin Costner's character in *WaterWorld* — is more likely to be found than a land-based one. Bigfoot hasn't been found. True believers can hoot, holler, pound their candy-wrapper-littered desks with righteous indignation and implore non-believers to study the proof. They can watch the Patterson-Gimlin film over and over, looking for the glint of zipper and never see it, never really look for it, because gazing into your own psychosis is mind-bending. It is the most frightening expedition of all.

That's the real reason why Spinner, Christine, and I turned down the invitation for the post-Bigfoot finding beer fest and sweaty body celebration. One would think that any male or female horndog would enjoy flirting with the opposite sex in a cabin stuck in the middle of a national forest. But like Caligula's court, the scent and sweat of madness becomes exhausting. I imagine male and female expedition-goers lying side-by-side in a bulging oversized sleeping bag, smoking cigarettes and whispering intimately about how Bigfoot had brought them together; that somewhere in the cosmos a deity had appointed Bigfoot as their matchmaker ... and then discussing how they were going to hide their scandalous relationship from their spouse, scheduling their next rendezvous for the following expedition.

Every cult has its customs, its initiations, and its unrealistic faith in something unexplainable. Every cult has its apostles, its sects, and offshoots from the main core. Every cult constantly searches for enlightenment. Every cult has its zealous few, the mainstream population, and those not yet fully convinced. Every cult must convert others to survive and self-perpetuate through promises of exaltation, soulful discovery, enlightenment.

Every cult has its prophet.

Spinner, Christine, and I sat in the Kalaloch Lodge hotel room on the last night of our stay. We didn't talk much as we packed our things. I loaded Mel's story tapes in my military bag. Four hours of stories, all about Bigfoot or phantoms. Getting late.

A knock at the door. I opened it.

It was the EL.

He smiled. Spinner glanced at him and then sat down on his bed. Christine welcomed him with a dreary smile. I shook his hand, smiled like a politician, and got him a chair.

He sat down.

"We're over at my cabin," said the EL. "Having a party. Want to join us?"

"Nah," I said. "These long nights wore us out."

Christine nodded in agreement. Spinner just stared.

"Was Mel here?" asked the EL.

"Yeah," I said.

"What did he want?" The EL leaned forward, as if I were going to relay something of great import.

"Nothing," I said. "He told us stories."

"Oh," said the EL. He leaned back. "What did you think about the expedition?"

"It was interesting."

"Pretty scary, huh? Down there along the river?"

"It was," I said. "Smelled like dead fish."

"That happens a lot. First-timers have encounters, and they get hooked. Come back again and again. It's exciting. But don't worry. Bigfoot is harmless. They've evolved to stay clear of humans."

"Obviously," I said with a smile.

Spinner opened a Coke can. It fizzed.

"Come on over to the get-together," said EL. "It's a good time."

"I'm bushed. We gotta catch a plane tomorrow morning. Long flight back to Pennsylvania."

"Okay," said the EL. "So what did you think ... overall?"

"Well, to be honest, I expected more in the way of an *expedition*. I appreciate the Bigfoot knowledge, but it seems the planning could have been better."

The EL didn't blink. He changed his face from curious openness to earnestness. "We're working on that. This is new to a lot of people. They don't understand that looking for Bigfoot is more of a group thing than a single person with night-vision goggles sitting in the woods. But a lot of people saw and heard things they couldn't explain."

"Like red eye shine," I said.

"Yep," said the EL. "We did see that."

"*We* didn't see it," said Christine. "Others saw it."

The EL nodded, but it was an ambiguous nod, not agreeing with Christine, not repudiating her either. A practiced nod; if I smiled like a politician, then he nodded like a politician.

"Would you go on another Bigfoot hunt?" asked the EL.

"If it were closer and less expensive, then maybe," I said. I did not want to alienate the EL. Even with my suspicions that this was an absolute farce, there was a chance that the EL's intentions were somewhat pure. Plus, to be selfish, the believers I met during the expedition provided excellent fodder for my upcoming book. My imagination, which I believe to be prodigious, could not have conjured up those individuals who beat the bush for Bigfoot.

"How about you, Spinner?" asked the EL.

"No," said Spinner. He chuckled. "I don't think so."

The EL sighed. He stood tall. "Thanks for coming. I'll see you all in the morning."

We said our goodbyes. The EL left, closing the door softly behind him. Christine, Spinner, and I sat in silence for a while, lost in thoughts of Bigfoot orgies, drunken groupies, Native American tales, and plane rides.

Spinner broke the silence. "Why do you lead the guy on?"

I shrugged. "I don't know. Self-interest?"

"You're too nice," said my lovely wife. "You know what he's about. But you give him the benefit of the doubt. It's just you."

"I guess it's just me," I said.

"This whole thing smells like dead fish." Spinner finished his soda.

"I'm ready to go home," I said.

SIX DEGREES
OF BIGFOOT SEPARATION

Home. Work. Life. I was convinced that my Bigfoot expedition days were over. I continued to be embarrassed about the financial cost of a badly organized and farcical expedition. For three months after I returned, I compiled notes and cruised Bigfoot chat rooms. It was at this time that I internalized the religious fervor of those that believe in Bigfoot, Sasquatch, Queventelliur, Stick People, etc. Bigfoot believers separated themselves into camps or "sects." These sects are usually at odds with one another, declaring their "rightness" with chest-thumping (pun intended) proclamations about Bigfoot's origins. All sects claim that the other sects are misguided, sometimes insane, maybe corrupt, and/or just stupid. Gossip about love trysts, fraud, and criminal behavior dominate their respective chat rooms. After navigating this metaphysical mess, I identified four distinct Bigfoot belief systems.

1. Bigfoot as a purely biological entity (BE)[5]

Those in the BE camp believe Bigfoot to be a missing link, a completely separate evolutionary humanoid

---

5   I could create a 5th sect, those BE believers that are convinced that Bigfoot utilizes psychic ability (evolved over millennia) and infrasound to intimidate humans. However; I placed this system underneath the BE umbrella.

(like Gigantopithecus Blacki or Homo Erectus) or some other type of great American ape that is not Gigantopithecus Blacki. Bigfoot is provable from a biological standpoint, in that it is simply a living, breathing creature that can be categorized by genus and species. BE believers have hypothesized that Bigfoot has gluten allergies (DO NOT FEED THE BIGFOOT PEANUT BUTTER AND JELLY!), migrates during the seasons, and speaks in a guttural sort of pseudo-Asiatic language called Samurai. Bigfoot is attracted to the smell of cooking bacon and raids dumpsters for food. Bigfoot is territorial and marks its trails and territory by snapping limbs or pushing over young trees. Bigfoot builds basic shelters of sticks and plant matter and lives in family groups. Some claim to have found Bigfoot feces, long massive turds that resemble human turds. Closet scatologists examine these whopper turds, searching for clues to its diet. They claim that no known animal could produce cylindrical-like turds, and that no known human has an asshole the size of a softball.

2. *Bigfoot as a member of the Guardian Alliance (GA) – a psychic Bigfoot (as related by all-seeing percipients)*

The GA view is summarized earlier in this book. The Queventelliur/Bigfoot race is part of the Guardian Alliance (GA) that monitors the earth for some cosmic reason. The whole dogma surrounding the guardian alliance, intruders and the entire Inter-dimensional Associations of Free Worlds is so bizarre and convoluted that a quick synopsis does not suffice. For an in-depth understanding, I suggest reading all writings by Ashayana Deane and her mate Azurtanya Deane. My best guess is that the "Psychic Bigfoot" or Queventelliur" is the hirsute inter-dimensional long jumper that acts as a lookout for Guardian races such as the Aethian, Rhanthunkeana, Breneau and mixed-race mutts developed through extensive inter-breeding. The GA protects us carbon-based weak ass humans from fallen angelic legions or intruders, evil time and dimension manipulators like the Annunaki, Zephelium and Dracos. By the way, the Dracos used the Dinosaurs as lookouts and created the Chupacabra. Presumably all this information comes straight to Deane from the guardians of Earth's Planetary Templar Complex. These guardians float about in Harmonic Universe 2 and occasionally make the trip here to speak to those worthy of their guidance[6].

3. *Bigfoot as an Extra-Terrestrial (ET)*

Many believe that Bigfoot is an alien species, a benevolent environmentalist sent to earth to educate us loathsome humans. These hairy hominids are dropped off by their alien friends, most likely humanoid UFO pilots with far less hair than their cousins, to roam about in the forests. People report strange lights in connection with Bigfoot sightings and Bigfoot "sounds"

---

6   If you feel that reading all of Deane's books is a chore, try https://www.emeraldguard-ians.nl.eu.org/p/keylontic-dictionary.html as a source for Deane's teachings. The link between Keylontic Science, Bigfoot, Aliens and QAnon can also be found.

(humming, beeping, thumping, clanging, thunderous farting, etc.), an odd concurrence of events that led many to believe that Bigfoot is a cosmic hitchhiker. This massive ET communicates with special people that interpret "alienese" much better than the rest of us mortals. Stick signs, ripped-apart animals, and symbols scraped in the dirt are actually complicated cryptic communiqués[7]. Men in Black (MIB) have been associated with these Bigfoot sightings. Like the Queventelliur of the Harmonic Universes, these creatures can disappear if pursued. A famous incident of repeated UFO and Bigfoot encounters is reported to have happened in Pennsylvania, 1973[8]. Bigfoot ETs have visited the earth for a million years and co-existed with our more human-like ancestors. Those who encounter the alien version of Bigfoot report "missing time" phenomenon, and some claim to contact these Bigfoot alien forms on a regular basis and are referred to as Bigfoot contactees (one wonders if Bigfoot likes to probe his contactees). There are numerous books about "Bigfoot as alien theory," but the most lucid explanation of the Bigfoot/alien connection is found on the TV series the *Six Million Dollar Man* in the two-part episode titled "The Secret of Bigfoot." A fantastic summary of this episode can be found on the Bionic Wiki (http://bionic.wikia.com/wiki/The_Secret_of_Bigfoot). The Bionic Wiki summary is as follows:

---

7   Lisa A. Shiel offers a detailed treatise on the UFO Bigfoot connection in her non-fiction book: *Backyard Bigfoot – The True Story of Stick Signs, UFOs and the Sasquatch.* And yes, I read the whole damn thing!

8   Detailed information on these Bigfoot UFO encounters can be found at https://www.stan-gordon.info/wp/. Reference materials for these encounters are also found on the website.

Steve Austin and Oscar Goldman are in a remote region of the California mountains as part of a team working with high tech earthquake sensors. Two geologists--Ivan and Marlene Bekey--disappear in mysterious circumstances. Tracks of the legendary wild beast called Sasquatch or Bigfoot are found nearby. Ivan is soon found safe but in a state of shock. However, there is no sign of Marlene. When Bigfoot later attacks the team's base camp Steve pursues and fights with the beast, unaware that he is being monitored by aliens living in a nearby mountain. During the fight one of Bigfoot's arms becomes detached, revealing that it is not an animal but some form of robot. Bigfoot flees (complete with the removed arm!) and Steve follows it into a cave. This turns out to be inside the mountain occupied by the aliens and Steve is soon rendered unconscious, captured and analyzed.

When he awakes, Steve learns from Shalon - a female alien - that Bigfoot was built and controlled by the aliens to protect them. The earthquake sensor team was attacked as they identified a volcanic vent that powered the alien colony. Meanwhile Oscar learns that a major earthquake is predicted along the main San Andreas fault line within the next few hours, which jeopardizes all the Californian west coast cities. Only a controlled underground nuclear explosion to trigger a smaller man-made earthquake along a smaller tributary fault line will prevent the main earthquake from happening. Oscar authorizes this knowing that Steve and Marlene are still missing and will be at serious risk from the explosion and subsequent earthquake.

This episode of the *Six Million Dollar Man* matches the basic premise that Bigfoot is, indeed, an alien. Bigfoot is our interstellar professor, although this dynamo of natural wisdom shows himself only to certain types.

4. *Bigfoot as a Native American Magic Man (MM)*

From what I've gathered from interviews and research, Native Americans do believe in Bigfoot as a "magic man." Bigfoot can lead one astray and is a protector of the wilderness, similar to beliefs espoused by those who think Bigfoot is interstellar or interdimensional. A common theme is that of otherworldly environmentalist or pseudo-supernatural being, as if Bigfoot in its numerous Native American forms (and there are hundreds of names for the Bigfoot creature) exists as an "earth brother." I have had the opportunity to talk to tribe members who pray to the spirits for protection from these creatures whenever they explore the wilderness of their native Washington State. Yakama elders revere Bigfoot and are wary about any man, white or otherwise, who dares attempt to track and find these magical creatures. Following is a quote from a Yakama tribe member: "This thing that's out here, it's got a lot of medicine, it's got a lot of power to it. Spiritually, they can take you." I have to argue with anyone who suggests that Native American mythology does not support the existence of a hairy protector of the wilderness. I suspect that peyote had, and has, something to do with seeing Bigfoot, but I also suspect that Bigfoot is one of those common memes that seep into culture; a meme[9] spreads like a cultural virus through centuries and evolves into an intricate belief system. This meme has mutated. Bigfoot is viewed as biological by some Native Americans, inter-dimensional by others, and a combination of the two by many more. It is interesting that Native American myth encapsulates the whole of the other doctrines, that of the BE, UFO, and GA Bigfoot beliefs. A fascinating account of the Spokane Tribe and Bigfoot is written in the diary of Elkanah Walker circa 1840. You can find much of that information on http://www.bigfootencounters.com/classics/walker.htm References to the diary entries are posted there.

I'm amazed by the number of devotees to each of the beliefs. Expeditions to find each type of Bigfoot are offered for reasonable fees by various organizations, including those organizations that believe Bigfoot to be an ET or traveler through the Harmonic Universes. Underneath the BE umbrella, multiple regional organizations offer guided expeditions (these can be found in Texas, Washington, Pennsylvania, New York, Canada, etc.). I could not find a specific Native American expedition, most likely because Native Americans insist that searching for the magic man could result in death. Although curious about what type of person believes in mystical or UFO-based

---

9   For more information on memes and how they affect culture and belief systems read *Breaking the Spell* by Daniel C. Dennet.

Bigfoots, I could not justify attending any more expeditions, much less actually paying for the privilege of listening to those who claim first-hand knowledge on dimension-jumping Bigfoots, UFO-riding Bigfoots, or Bigfoots that can curse people with their eyes. Even with my innate ability to feign interest and a reasonable open-mindedness to ridiculous concepts (I work inside the federal government, for God's sake) I could no longer pretend to give these theories credence. Searching for unicorns, centaurs, dragons, leprechauns, Thunderbirds, fairies, or Butterfly Gods would be at least an equally valuable use of my time.

Sorry, Grandpa. I could not initially prove that the Mighty Peculiar was indeed Sasquatch. If I listened to those that believed in Queventelliur, I couldn't prove the damn thing existed anyway. Like some hairy, smelly Dorothy from Oz, it would just blink twice and click its heels together so that it could disappear through a dimensional portal and land in a Harmonic Universe--maybe sip tea with one of the Alien Grays.

I was done with Bigfoot expeditions. Kaput!

Imagine my surprise when months later the expedition leader called my home and invited me on another expedition, to a state park in West Virginia that bordered the Monongahela National Forest, the very place where I had first encountered the Mighty Peculiar.

Mentioning that I worked in the NSA finally came back to haunt me.

"Want to go?" asked the EL.

"No," I said. "Why invite me anyway?"

"An ESPN reporter will be there," said the EL. "He asked about you."

"How does he know about me?" I must have sounded incredulous.

"Remember Chuck?"

"Yes," I answered. Warily. Chuck's faith in Bigfoot had astounded Christine, Spinner, and me at the Kalaloch Lodge.

"He's friends with the ESPN guy. He told his buddy that a guy from the NSA is searching for Bigfoot. That guy is you."

"That's funny," I said. "I'm only a defense contractor now."

"It would help me out if you came along," said the EL.

"Too expensive," I said. "Nothing personal, but it isn't worth it."

"No cost to you. You're there as my guest."

"OK," I said after a moment of contemplation. "I'll do it."

"Can he interview you?"

"Sure," I said. "What's his name?"

"Don Barone."

"Never heard of him," I said. "I'll check him out." (Little did I know that Don Barone was checking me out too).

"He's legit," said the EL. "Emmys."

JIM JONES HAD CHARISMA

I drove through valleys and mountain passes, a meandering five-hour drive from my suburban home in southern Pennsylvania to the sparsely populated county of Pocahontas in West Virginia, gateway to Watoga State Park on the southern tip of the Monongahela National Forest. I'm familiar with West Virginia terrain, and the irony is not lost on me that Bigfoot first entered my life on the other side of the Monongahela Forest, almost straight north. When I arrived, I experienced an overwhelming sense of Sasquatch *déjà vu*. The campground stretched to the edge of the Greenbrier River, an almost eerie East Coast twin to the campground in Washington State. Bigfoot enthusiasts wandered about, some sipping coffee from mugs, others gripping beer cans. They all laughed and talked with easy familiarity, a closeness about them that I almost envied. Secure in their knowledge of Bigfoot's existence, they could enjoy each other's opinions without fear of reprisal. Here and there, a campfire crackled in the early evening. In the center of the campground a large three-quarter-ton truck with a tow-behind trailer acted as the Bigfoot Command Post (CP). Antennae sprouted from the top of the tow-behind. A retired Army sergeant and his wife had volunteered their long-range hand-held radios and base station to the EL. The EL did not have a tent amongst the clientele. He rented a cabin.

Spinner accompanied me once again. His drive from Michigan had been much longer than mine. Thankfully, he brought with him a massive tent, complete with cooking stoves and ample supplies for a week, even though we were scheduled to stay only three days. He was already well on his way to completing the tent set-up. Spinner waited for no man, and I was mostly useless anyhow when it came to getting our gear together. I hopped out of my truck. Spinner and I embraced with an awkward man hug and mumbled, "Hey dude." It had been seven months since Olympic National Forest and the dead fish episode.

Turning around, I noticed a gaggle of humanity approaching. In the center, the unmistakable silhouette of the EL; although not morbidly obese, his considerable size and girth dwarfed that of his minions. He was literally the center of attention, with equal numbers flanking his left and right—a phalanx of believers. He approached me as royalty would approach a distinguished guest of the kingdom. Although not subservient, I attempted to be gracious, almost honored by his personal and genuine greeting. His "privy chamber" followers expected respect from me. That, I would not give.

"Here he comes," I said to Spinner.

"Fat-ass," mumbled Spinner. I wasn't sure if Spinner referred to me or the EL. It was funny either way.

The EL frowned slightly when he realized that Spinner sat by the fire. But Spinner's presence did not stop the EL from shaking my hand and his. Spinner's sinister smile might appear benevolent to some, but it didn't fool me. I'm not sure if the EL failed to recognize Spinner's contempt or chose to ignore it.

"May I speak with you in private?" the EL asked.

I nodded. The EL shooed away his followers, placed his hand on my shoulder and led me away from the campfire, toward the river bank. He wanted to separate me from the others to mask our conversation with the river's noise, made louder by the previous night's hard rain.

We stopped only steps from the water's edge. I imagined that one simple slip, or shove, into the fast-moving water might result in a soggy, quick death. I kept him in front of me. Just in case.

The EL tossed a rock into the water. "What do you think he will ask?"

"Who?"

"The reporter." The EL seemed perturbed.

I really didn't know, so I said, "I don't know."

The EL shoved his hands in his pockets and stared intently across the river. He was pondering a sensitive subject, no doubt. So I gave him time to gather his thoughts. I was curious. He turned toward me and closed the distance with a quick step in my direction. In a low voice, he asked, "Will you tell me exactly what the ESPN reporter asks you or tells you? I don't want him to take anything out of context."

"What could he take out of context?"

"It's easy to twist words."

"I don't believe that this reporter cares much about disproving Bigfoot or making anyone here look stupid," I said. "This is just a human-interest story."

"I've been burned before," said the EL.

Although I had read disparaging remarks about the EL on multiple forums, I did not believe that the ESPN reporter, Don Barone, had any intention of exposing the EL as a charlatan. Chuck, the true believer that Spinner and I befriended in Washington, was a generous contributor (a curator or something of that sort) to the EL's organization. It had been Chuck who told Don about me, and Don wouldn't embarrass his close friend (a quick analysis I made with limited information). Chuck's motive, I believe, was to give the EL's organization positive press through the world's largest sports network. An entrepreneur by nature, Chuck saw the EL's organization as a combination of adventure camping, research institute, and social clique, an educational and profitable private club. I could never question Chuck's conviction about Bigfoot's existence. His pronouncement to Christine, Spinner and me months before at the Kalaloch Lodge stuck with me:

"Faith," said Chuck. He waved his fork at us, a piece of syrup-slimed pancake impaled on its end. "We're going to find Bigfoot."

"I don't know your history," I said.

"I just want to find Bigfoot," said the EL. "Really. That's all I want people to say about me. I'm here to educate. That's all."

"Okay," I said.

"Please, let me know what he asks you. Let me know what you tell him. And, if you hear anything else ...."

The EL's attempt to control information set off gong-sized alarm bells in my head. I wasn't sure why he trusted me with his worries, but he lost the benefit of my doubt. I understood his caution about releasing certain data to the "public" on the inner workings of his organization and releasing details about sightings and video evidence in his collection, but his hubris in attempting to stage-manage how people responded to questions astounded me. Manipulating his followers was one thing, but now the EL counted me as a confidant, and quite possibly, a fellow traveler. So, I smiled and nodded my head.

"I'll let you know exactly what Don Barone asks me," I replied. "I'll tell him you're a man who believes in Bigfoot and wants people to know the truth."

"Thanks." The EL sighed, visibly relieved.

"You're welcome," I said.

The EL slapped my back and walked away. As soon as he entered the light of the campfires his followers swarmed to him like moths to a bright light ... or bug zapper.

I sat down beside Spinner. He passed me a bag of beef jerky. I chewed on it awhile.

Finally, Spinner asked, "Did you drink the Kool-Aid?"

"Yeah," I answered.

"This is damn weird, doing this again."

"Yeah," I said. "It is." I poked around in the fire with a stick. "He wants me to tell him what people say about him. He coached me on what to say to the ESPN reporter."

"You surprised?" asked Spinner.

"DB"

Silver and staid, a Toyota minivan stopped across from our campsite. At first, I paid little attention, but the EL rushed to the Toyota as if it held a case of filet mignon. The minivan driver was either a caterer or the ESPN reporter. I waited for a robust, ruddy type to leap from the driver's seat, to begin fist-pumping the expedition goers while simultaneously cinching his steel-frame backpack for that long hike in the woods. ESPN, I assumed, would send an outdoors-savvy individual to survive the rigors of all-night Bigfoot hunting and sleep deprivation.

With wary circumspection, Bigfoot expedition-goers circled the van. Like dogs sniffing another dog's ass, they wrinkled their noses and squinted eyes in anticipation of Don Barone's appearance. I shouldn't have been surprised at their collective reaction. Possibly — probably — the EL had warned his followers of the potential for bad press. A misplaced word could jeopardize *good* press and turn a positive into a perpetual negative. The EL's livelihood, obviously, depended on those willing to pay for the expertise of his curators and trackers. Impressing the reporter was a huge part of the EL's marketing plan. I didn't hold that against him. A good businessman recognizes that a positive story, either in print or on television, from the ESPN media leviathan would cement his credibility. Credibility translates into clientele willing to invest in a product, whether as customers or bona fide business partners.

It must be extremely difficult to build a business model around the search for and/or worship of mythical creatures. I had yet to find an adventure camp that searched for werewolves or the Jersey Devil (aside from tours conducted by the park service as a lark). The EL had to constantly manipulate perception so that Bigfoot was not lumped into a category reserved for chupacabras, unicorns, minotaurs, lake monsters, thunderbirds and Amazon women. His organization must appear professional and reputable. Which means, by God, that Bigfoot does exist if one searches for it. *I search therefore* It *exists*--some warped Cartesian view that people must buy into with heart and soul.

The van door opened, opposite me. The EL walked to the driver's side. I waited. I could not see Don Barone. Spinner walked over and stood beside me.

"How much ass you think he's kissing?" asked Spinner.

I puckered up and made sucking sounds.

"Yeah," said Spinner. "Maybe." Spinner did not sound convinced.

"You don't think he's kissing ass?"

"A little. He's got such a huge ego. He probably expects the ESPN guy to kiss *his* ass."

"Yeah," I said. "Maybe."

Then Don Barone appeared.

He was no outdoors type. He shuffled around the van using a cane. His hair sprung from the sides of his ball cap like gray wires. I saw a bong-smoking hippie wearing cargo pants, a washed- out Hawaiian shirt and a twenty-five-dollar pair of ruggedized sneakers that one buys at a wannabe camping store. Gargoyle sunglasses hung from his neck. A slight squint to his eyes and upturned corner of mouth indicated a man who had seen it all but still couldn't quite comprehend why the crazies acted crazy. The Bigfoot expedition goers closed in, craning their necks to see the man from ESPN, an investigative reporter who looked like a slightly younger brother to David Crosby from Crosby, Stills and Nash, a gimp with an attitude and a cynic's smile. I expected him to break out into a raspy rendition of "Southern Cross." I didn't approach him but simply watched as a tide of true believers crested at his minivan. Euphoria infected the crowd, barely uncontained exhilaration at Bigfoot's opportunity to become the next big story, an accepted part of American life, a pop culture superhero representing all that's right about human concern for nearly extinct animals and earth's fragile environment.

Spinner and I wandered back to the fire. Night rapidly approached and searching for the monster would begin in only a few short hours. I drank soda. Caffeine helps on long nights. A couple of Bigfoot-believing females stopped by our campfire. I knew one of them already.

"Hi, Denver," said Sap. Sap's friend held a beer.

"Hello," I said.

Sap's friend stood directly behind me.

"Nice big tent," said Sap's friend. Her glassy-eyed stare and fluttering smile scared the holy living crap out of me.

Spinner raised an eyebrow, then stuck a wiener on a stick. He hummed "Row, Row, Row Your Boat."

106

"Thanks," I said. "Sleeps five."

"Where's the wife?" asked Sap. She ignored Spinner, like most of the Bigfoot crowd. They did not like him, with him being an asshole and all.

"Home," I said. I might have been mistaken, but the women seemed to inch closer to the campfire. I also realized that my participation in this expedition *sans* wife could be sending signals to Bigfoot groupies that I was available for a hooting and hollering *praise be to Bigfoot* night of chest-banging goings-on. This was assuredly not the case. The uneasy feeling that crawled along my spine almost validated my hypothesis that Bigfoot expeditions were about "oh so much more" than proving Bigfoot's existence through photographic and/or auditory evidence. It was about wieners on sticks. It was about pecker length, mating habits, and screams in the night. But an uneasy feeling does not constitute evidence of the goings-on, and I had no real evidence of sexual shenanigans.

"There's gonna be some long nights," slurred Sap's friend.

"Sure are," I said. "You know, with us looking for Bigfoot ..."

Her toothy grin lit up the night--neon Chiclets. "Long nights," she repeated. Sap's friend was two beers away from extended sleepy time.

Sap patted my shoulder. "Are you going out with me and Mel tonight?"

"Probably tomorrow," I said. "I'm supposed to talk with the ESPN guy."

"Isn't this exciting?" asked Sap. "ESPN is here!"

I expected her to clap her hands together and jump up and down.

Sap's friend promptly forgot about me. She looked over

her shoulder toward the silver minivan and the milling throng surrounding it and then wandered slowly back up the road, visions of ESPN reporters maybe floating in her head. From this distance, and in the gloom, I imagined the throng to be zombies from *Night of the Living Dead*.

Sap sat down.

"Don't you want to hang out with your friend?" asked Spinner.

"She can take care of herself," snapped Sap.

Spinner hummed "Mary Had a Little Lamb" now. I almost laughed. To have someone that brazen and irritating on my side gave me a warm fuzzy. The image of Spinner humming nursery rhymes and roasting wieners is imprinted forever in my mind.

Spinner, Sap, and I sat quietly. Nothing much to say, and I didn't know how to break the silence. Spinner bailed me out.

"Here he comes," said Spinner. "Weird-looking dude."

Don Barone limped toward us, agonizingly slow. The Bigfoot zombies peeled away as he closed the gap on our campfire. No doubt, the Bigfoot zombies wanted to stay clear of Spinner. I'm reasonably sure they did not feel welcome in our circle--and for the most part, they were correct. Plus, I'm guessing every expedition participant was aware that Spinner worked as a state trooper and might pack heat. It's also plausible that they of the true believer ilk felt reasonably confident that if they pissed Spinner off, he would remove said heat and shoot them directly in the hind parts. Knowing Spinner for years, I can confidently pronounce that Spinner would do no such thing. He wouldn't shoot them; he would kill them quietly and then bury them beneath a large tree somewhere[10].

I stood to greet Don. I reached out and shook his hand. "Need a chair?"

"Uh, yeah," said Don. "Hip hurts like hell."

As he sat, I asked, "Hip replacement?"

Don nodded. "It's a bitch."

I liked him immediately.

Spinner walked over and introduced himself.

"You must be the state trooper," said Don. "Chuck told me."

Spinner nodded.

Don reached over and shook Sap's hand. Sap quickly gave her name and then said two words that irritated me: "Bigfoot researcher."

Research. Common Sense. Interviewing. Perspective. The ability to ferret out the outlandish from the reasonable is a trait I try to cultivate. I fail at times—never eat a Big Mac when driving a stick shift—but I'm more or less a capable researcher and at least possess an adequate bullshit meter. After speaking with Bigfoot enthusiasts/researchers and those who filmed the creature (Bob Gimlin) I think that most who believe that they witnessed Bigfoot, found tracks, or heard strange sounds were innocent victims of hoaxes, lacked perspective- -or had experienced something unexplainable. However, there are men and women who hoax sightings and evidence to gain notoriety for the express purpose of making money. These men and women are the ultimate pyramid-marketing

---

10   This is, of course, a joke. Spinner is a professional. He just gives off a certain "vibe" like Lewis (played by Burt Reynolds) from the movie *Deliverance*.

racketeers, snake oil salesmen of the most convincing kind. It takes tremendous talent to persuade people with even average intelligence that a seven-foot-plus tall monster shits in the woods. It takes a maestro of information to persuade otherwise frugal individuals to pay large sums of money to search during moonlit nights for a flesh- and-blood Native American legend. A Bigfoot believer who convinces people to spend money on expeditions that hunt for a Queventelliur/ psychic Bigfoot that can navigate at will between Harmonic Universes is genius! What would one use to capture such a creature — a nuclear accelerator from *Ghostbusters*? "Don't cross the streams!"

Although Sap irritated me with the Bigfoot researcher comment, I liked Sap. She seemed sincere, in a fawning kind of way. She was an innocent victim. A true believer. She sang to Bigfoot. She sketched pictures of Bigfoot. She might like to imbibe a bit while singing to Bigfoot, but don't we all?

But let's call the Bigfoot entrepreneurs what they are: businessmen, businesswomen, marketers, and/or charlatans. I might stumble into naiveté by saying that some researchers are sincere, like Sap. There is nothing wrong with making money--as long as intentions are honorable, evidence is substantiated (by whatever means mythic evidence can be substantiated) and those in control are reputable. If free-thinking souls want to pay for petrified lumps of unicorn stool and those selling the stool are convinced that they are, indeed, selling petrified unicorn stool, there is nothing wrong with that. People spend money on ridiculous items and services all the time. Hell, people pay to marry their dogs to other dogs.

Only a few Bigfoot "entrepreneurs" are frauds. These frauds hoax pictures, video, or evidence. Money is the motive, and fame is the bonus, in my humble opinion. It's a cult of personality based on something unprovable.

But it would be cool if Bigfoot existed. Spinner thought the same way. I think Don Barone thought that, too. The unprovable did not rule out hope for something outrageous. Discovering evidence that makes Bigfoot a mere possibility would be exhilarating.

Fires flickered; the Greenbrier River's dark water rushed by, only forty yards distant.

"Do you believe in Bigfoot?" Don looked at me, so I figured I should answer first.

"Not really," I said.

"No," said Spinner.

Sap stayed quiet.

"A lot of people say they saw Bigfoot," said Don. "You think they lied?"

I shrugged.

"People like attention," said Spinner.

"It's hard to believe that every person lied," said Don.

"I don't think that," I said. "I do believe that people see what they want to see."

Don contemplated for a moment. "Not all of them were looking for Bigfoot."

"True," I said. "I don't have an answer for that... completely. But I know that the first time I saw a satellite, I thought it was a UFO driven by aliens. I do think that the mind replays common cultural images when it can't categorize something...like stuff from television and books."

"Why are you out here, then?" asked Don. "Being a former NSA guy?"

"A few reasons. I'm researching a novel; the people out here are perfect characters for my book. I like the mystery of it, too. There's really not much stuff that we are going to find new in this world, and if there is actually some big hairy biped walking around out there, I'd like to see it for myself." I then added, "Plus, I want to prove my grandfather isn't crazy."

"So, there's no top-secret government agency hiding a Bigfoot somewhere?" Don smiled when he asked me this.

"Not that I know of." I smiled when I replied.

"That would be a good story," said Don.

"I wish it were true. I want Bigfoot to exist."

"Is your grandfather crazy?"

"No, I don't think so." I then told Don the story of the spring line, about the loud crashing thingamajig that chased Grandpa and me all the way to our hunting trailer.

"You think it was Bigfoot?" asked Don.

"Don, I don't even know if I remember everything correctly. Who knows? There are so many other things in the woods. Bigfoot is not the default creature I would use to explain that noise, or anything else that happens in the woods."

My comment about Bigfoot as the *default* explanation for the unexplainable turned out to be prescient.

Sap finally said with a small voice, "Bigfoot is real."

Don asked, "How do you know?"

"I've seen Bigfoot three times. It's drawn to me for some reason."

"Really?"

"Yes. I believe it's attracted to women more than men."

I had heard this line of reasoning before. I did not agree. If Bigfoot existed as a breeding species, wouldn't there be a roughly equal proportion of males to females? Why wouldn't female Bigfoots be attracted to men singing bar tunes? Or men pissing in the woods? And, if Bigfoot had evolved to such a state as to be so surreptitious that human technology and effort could not locate it, why would Bigfoot jeopardize its safety by visiting singing, laughing humans? Sap honestly believed that her singing, along with reassuring psychic vibes that women emit, entice the creatures to come in close for a look-see. Bigfoot experts tell me that Bigfoot is curious. Bigfoot is lonely. Bigfoot might very well crave companionship. Great. Maybe so. But that does not marry up with the equal and competing argument that Bigfoot is so advanced in its woodsmanship that even multispectral, hyperspectral, and infrared technologies would fail to find the creature. Even the BE believers preach that Bigfoot is one with the woods. Hell, we're searching for Bigfoot in its own living room. It owns every crag and nook. It can hide its 500-pound body behind a young sapling. It utilizes shadows like a special operations soldier. It emits smells and infrasound to scare us pitiful humans. It protects its territory by throwing stones and marks boundaries with bent trees and stick signs.

But despite its advanced adaptations, Bigfoot just melts when he hears a soulful rendition of "I Will Always Love You."

The other theory posited about Bigfoot's attraction to women is bizarre and head scratching. Bigfoot, like men, is attracted to scent of a woman. However, the attraction becomes doubly strong when women menstruate (This is a real Bigfoot believer theory—and I'm almost uncomfortable writing about this). Bigfoot loves the smell of blood! Makes him a frisky devil! I was surprised that baiting Bigfoot with used tampons and sanitary napkins was a thing. I suppose to Bigfoot believers that would be akin to stacking a pile of naked wiggling Playboy Bunnies in the middle of New York City to attract human men. Males will sacrifice security and dignity for just a whiff of the attainable. A whitetail buck is the master of its domain, but come breeding time, the whitetail buck is clueless and single-minded in his pursuit to screw. Many hunters shoot whitetails during this frenetic breeding period. Would a Bigfoot jeopardize its safety for a chance to breed with a human? Bigfoot believers think so.

BIGFOOT NEEDS GOOD BOOTS

First full night of the West Virginia expedition and it was scary, sinister dark. The moon was a sliver, appearing in quick moments between clouds that drifted slowly overhead. Our search group queued in a parking area. Mel, the first in line, peered down a trail that led into a valley surrounded by imposing peaks. Don Barone was with us, sans metal walker, but hobbled and not terribly excited about hiking into thick woods without illumination. Most of our walking would be accomplished without flashlights--a conga line of intrepid souls searching for a hairy devil. The darkness rivaled that of Olympic Park in Washington. The thick canopy overhanging the trail guaranteed a sightless hike, and I only hoped we didn't follow the leader blindly over some unseen cliff, like two-legged, stumbling lemmings. Mel would attempt to call in the eastern version of Sasquatch … if the eastern version existed.

I guessed we would venture no further than a half mile from the SUVs and vans bunched in the parking lot. I was skeptical about finding any undiscovered North American ape this close to a road and on a trail used by countless hikers. However, Bigfoot experts assured me that Bigfoot enjoyed convenience when tromping through the woods.

Why wouldn't a highly adapted creature utilize the same trails that humans used? Deer and bears did it! Our highly adapted Bigfoot wouldn't dare stay in the center of the rough and almost uninhabitable Monongahela National Forest where a gaggle of humans would never seem him or her. No, Bigfoot would visit the parking areas and curiously show up to see why we dudes and ladies walked together, loudly, near a park entrance.

I felt like singing.

As we descended the trail, through switchbacks, around rocks, and underneath overhanging trees, the full extent of our stupidity hit me. Bigfoot was not our biggest threat. Clumsiness was. Don's hip must have ached. Our muttered cursing and scrapings canceled out any surreptitiousness we hoped to gain by walking in complete darkness. We were cows with bells on, announcing our arrival to every forest animal. Nervous giggles from some of the younger folks pierced the night like crow calls. Spinner and I stayed apart and behind the other searchers, chatting with Don and doing our best not to scoff at the operation. I didn't want to ruin Don's excitement. Turned out, Don had never been excited.

"This is ridiculous," whispered Don. "Why would Bigfoot be within miles of us?"

"Good question," I whispered back. "Bigfoot wouldn't."

"Unless he's lonely," said Spinner.

"SSSHHHH," said Mel from up front.

"I heard that Bigfoot is curious," Don limped badly now.

"Curious about women, mostly," Spinner said quietly.

"And we have some of those," I whispered.

"Great," said Don. "A horny Bigfoot."

"You okay?" I asked Don.

Don shook his head. "I can't go much farther."

The EL wanted to impress Don, since the EL was the movie star. As our crew hiked to the bottom of the valley, the EL and his closest friends set up a temporary camp on an opposing ridge. The EL hoped to create excitement by blasting Bigfoot calls into the night with a super-charged speaker system. Barred owls, coyotes, or even Bigfoot might respond. I still wondered how the EL and the experts knew what Bigfoot sounded like. There had never been an eyewitness account or a video of a Bigfoot clucking and screaming. The recorded, and then reproduced, noises were "allegedly" made by Bigfoot. So, logic would dictate that calls not proven or validated could be used to lure an undiscovered and — most likely — mythological creature.

I brought my unicorn whistle. Just in case.

Finally, we reached a bridge that crossed over a wide stream. Marsh grasses surrounded the stream, a tidy wetland in the center of rock formed by West Virginia Mountains. The wind picked up and the clouds scattered, allowing the sliver of moon to cast a faint glow on the full, leafy trees that bordered the stream. Tops of mountains highlighted against a brilliant star-filled sky took my breath away. There was complete silence for the first time--the giggling and mutterings ceased as all stared along the length of narrow valley tucked between steep hills, surrounded by deciduous trees and conifers.

"Fucking gorgeous," said Spinner. Spinner had a way of capturing those special moments.

"Did you hear that?" asked Mel. The whole group heard

his question. I heard people inhaling and then holding their breath. Mel directed his question at me.

"No," I said.

"Listen," said Mel.

And then I did hear it … a long, low moan from far away … maybe coming from the next ridge (see sentence above about the EL and his buddies setting up a call blaster. Not that I'm accusing anyone).

I worked myself to the front of the line.

Mel talked into his radio. "Was that you?"

The EL's voice answered back, "No. Wasn't us."

"Coyote," I suggested.

The line behind us stretched over the bridge and onto the trail, about fifty yards of people. Mel handed me his radio and inclined his head toward the tree line.

"You going in there?" I asked.

"Yes," said Mel. His tone was always sonorous.

"Want me or Spinner to go?"

"I can move faster and quieter alone," said Mel. "No offense."

Mel handed me his radio. Most of those behind us had not heard our conversation, due to their heated whisperings about the origin of the low, mysterious moan. Mel made a beeline to the woods and disappeared behind overlapping conifers. He was our ghost searching for Bigfoot, and most of the expedition-goers didn't have a clue that Mel had left the group.

Mel was an East Coast neophyte. He had conducted all his Bigfoot hunting on the West Coast, until now. I marveled at his courage. Walking alone into a dark forest after midnight is a bit nerve-wracking; I don't care who you are.

The group gathered behind us, some walking partway back up the trail for curiosity's sake. Others huddled together, pressing against each other to fight April's spring chill. We waited for Mel.

Billy, a teenage college student, tapped me on the shoulder. "Where's Mel?"

I pointed into the darkness. "There."

"That's crazy."

Billy's story:

Don, Spinner, and I befriended young Billy Fields (not his real name) on the first evening of the expedition. While we sat smoking and joking around an impressive campfire, waiting for our first hike, Billy emerged from his run-down compact parked alongside the camp road and plopped himself down in one of our folding chairs, like he was an old friend. He wasn't a big kid, but he was certainly in shape, and we believed him when he told us that he wrestled for West Virginia University. He asked who we were. Any nineteen-year-old male can get excited about ESPN, and Billy became rapturous when Don mentioned his occupation as an ESPN reporter.

"Bigfoot is in Pennsylvania." Billy said this with the same excitement as a kid would when talking about Santa and his reindeer.

"You saw him?" asked Don.

That was usually Don's first question to believers. Other than Sap, the Bigfoot whistler, every person answered Don in the negative.

"Not exactly," said Billy. "But I think I heard It. In Johnstown, Pennsylvania."

"Tell me about It," said Don.

"It was summertime, and me and my friend were lying on a trampoline out in his backyard. His house backs up to woods, so I'm lying there looking at the stars, getting cool, when suddenly we hear this noise in the woods. I'm thinking, *Great, a skunk*. Real devil animals ... hate them. So, we're lying there, about four or five feet off the ground, when all of a sudden we hear this bloodcurdling scream come from the woods, above us, like ten feet in the air. I mean, it was so loud. I never heard anything like it. It wasn't a skunk."

"I was frozen. Couldn't move for a second. I just knew that It was going to come out of the woods. Man, we jumped off that damn trampoline and ran into the house and told his father. His dad didn't seem to believe us. He just said, 'Go to sleep. Ain't anything out there but animals.'"

Billy laughed nervously. He shifted in his chair. He grabbed a stick and poked around in the fire. "Sometimes when I hear something that sounds like that scream, I get up and close my dorm drapes--and, dude, I live on the fourth floor of the dorm."

"You thought it was Bigfoot?" asked Don.

"What else could make a noise like that?"

"An owl," I suggested.

"It was too loud," said Billy. "It was right on the edge of the woods. I mean, I could *feel* it."

Billy's comment about feeling the roar, his bones rattling like hundreds of tuning forks, was a common experience for many Bigfoot ear-witnesses. Maybe the infrasound theory emerged from this nonsense about people feeling the guttural roar of a Bigfoot, experiencing it in a completely physical and psychical sense. Like its malodorous scent, Bigfoot employed its soul-taking bawl to frighten. Obviously, the Bigfoot scream was an intimidation technique, used in moments of extreme and immediate danger, like when stumbling upon two hairless humans lying on a trampoline in the middle of a semi-suburban backyard.

Billy's belief was sincere and naïve. We liked him for that. His hoopty-mobile doubled as his camper. He did not bring food, so we fed him the first night and the following days. He ate only a little. I chalked that up to his wrestler training. Billy told us he didn't have much money, but searching for Bigfoot was worth every cent. When asked by Don how much the Bigfoot expedition cost him, Billy answered that the EL cut him a sweet deal. For only $300, Billy could sleep in his vehicle, camp in a public area, and hike with others through the night on public property in Watoga State Park. Billy could experience people smacking trees with baseball bats to mimic the wood-knocking techniques of Bigfoot (everyone knows that Bigfoot families communicate by beating heavy branches against tree trunks). For his $300, Billy received information on Bigfoot tracking techniques, sound identification education and hypotheses on Bigfoot habitat and food sources from the EL and his expert curators. Billy was thrilled at the bargain. Don, Spinner, and I were horrified.

And where else could you hang out during the middle of the night, on a bridge, in a wilderness, searching for creatures with an ESPN reporter, an intelligence analyst, a state trooper, and a Native American that bugled for Bigfoot? Where else could you flirt with girls who are horny for Bigfoot, look through a Gen-3 night-vision monocular and eat steak cooked on a gas

121

burner? For Billy Fields this was Disney World, an outdoor nightclub, and a haunted hayride all wrapped into one big awesome, super sweet, hell-of-a-good-vacation package.

Billy's haunted hayride part of the trip was about to begin. On the bridge.

With Mel searching through brush and pines.

We waited with hushed expectation. Any second, Mel would release his Bigfoot roar. The wind picked up slightly, funneled through the gap, moving the treetops and creating that horror movie whisper of leaves rustling and thin branches creaking. Not so loud as to cover Mel's imminent Bigfoot scream, but enough background noise to change our hike from foolish to slightly spooky. With the faint light cast by the moon I imagined what we looked like to the animals and/or Bigfoot peeking at us from their hiding places, us silhouetted on the bridge, a gaggle of camouflage wearing idiots standing almost shoulder to shoulder, closing ranks against the night.

Behind us, Billy said, "Time to man up."

Minutes of quiet. Nothing stirred. Then, from the opposing ridge, another long, low moan. Was it call-blasting from the EL's site? Was Mel up that way? Expedition-goers murmured with excited whispers. Could Bigfoot be aware of our presence?

Mel's Bigfoot scream pierced the night. I jumped. Don jumped. Spinner mouthed, "Holy FUUUUCCCKKKK." Even the wind stopped.

Many more minutes passed. Then, ahead of us, rustling in the trees. A loud crash echoed through the hollow. Billy grabbed Don's arm.

"Oh my God, what is that?" asked Billy in a not-too-manly, shaky voice.

"Time to man up," said Don. Don hobbled to where Spinner and I stood at the other end of the bridge, facing the rustling and crashing sounds. Everyone else shrunk back, including Billy. The wrestler's earlier pronouncements of "manning up" and "going after Bigfoot" were vaporized by his fear. Only Spinner, Don, and I stood at the ready. Don would wield his metal cane like a sword. Spinner's Glock 9MM would bark and spit fire. I would employ our most powerful weapon—common sense. I was quite sure that some other animal made the noises. If not another bipedal creature, a bear, deer, opossum, or giant raccoon might be heading our way.

A dark shape emerged from the wood line--gasps from the men and women behind us. This was it! Bigfoot had responded to Mel's call, could not help but satisfy his curiosity by visiting with the humans on the bridge. Hopefully, it wasn't mating season.

The figure raised its hand in salutation.

The figure bent down to tie a boot.

As far as I knew, Red Wing did not make boots in Bigfoot's size.

Side note: Jack Links Beef Jerky uses Bigfoot brilliantly in their "Messin' with Sasquatch"® commercials. I would think boot manufactures would do the same thing. A camera follows Bigfoot as he tromps around in the woods with a huge pair of boots, splashes through deep puddles, side-hills along a steep slope, jumps over boulders and rocks and finally ends up kneeling behind a tree and then peeks

123

his head around the trunk to watch unsuspecting, giggling couples roasting weenies at a campsite. An announcer with a gravelly bass voice says, "Even Bigfoot wears [insert name of Shoe Company here] boots. Our boots stand up to the worst weather and the harshest climates. [Insert name of Shoe Company here] boots: Tough enough for Bigfoot—tough enough for sissy humans."

The figure finished tying its boot. It stood up. It waved again.

I turned toward the line of people behind us. "It's only Mel," I shouted.

The group expressed its relief by simultaneously sighing, giggling, and talking in excited whispers.

In the dark, I could see Mel's smile. He reached the end of the bridge.

"Did I scare them?" asked Mel.

"Yeah, you scared them. Especially Billy."

"He didn't man up?"

"Nope," I said. "The cripple did, though."

Don pointed his cane at Mel. "Even the old man with new hips was ready."

Static from the radio hanging on Mel's belt. Mel fumbled it out of the holster.

From the radio, the EL's voice asked, "Did you see anything?"

"No," said Mel. "No real good food sources, either. I don't think this is a promising area."

"We heard something up here," said the EL.

"Sure it wasn't me?" asked Mel.

No answer from the EL. Mel holstered his radio after a

minute and stared back into the forest. Everyone became quiet, expecting some profound pronouncement.

Billy ran up to us and slapped Mel on the back. "That was fucking awesome! Holy shit!"

That was the pinnacle of profundity.

BIGFOOT PEOPLE SAY (AND DO) THE WEIRDEST THINGS

While researching this book, I cruised many Bigfoot forums and blogs. Several of the topics are, and were, so outlandish that I had to include them in this book. Of all the Bigfoot forums, the largest and most well established seems to be the Bigfoot Forums (BFF) found at www. bigfootforums.com. I've met many people through the forum that are intelligent, witty, sincere, and committed. I also swapped posts with combative, myopic, silly, sexually frustrated, hypocritical, dishonest, ignorant, and rude believers.

I'm sure there are private, closeted Bigfoot forums on the net also. Possibly, another stratum of subculture under the Bigfoot cultural umbrella concentrates on Bigfoot sexual habits and mating seasons. I wouldn't be surprised if there are people out there who mimic the alleged sexual practices of Bigfoot and that pay-to-play private forums are used as a dating service. What I and others witnessed on multiple expeditions could be characterized as humorous, but also somewhat disturbing. The last chapter in this book is a story written by Don Barone (with me as a co-author) on coordinating and executing a private Bigfoot expediton in the Adirondacks, where we invited true believers to accompany us. It was then I realized that the Bigfoot subculture existed far beyond what I imagined. Hundreds of thousands of people believe in Bigfoot. Many cannot help themselves when it comes to expressing their desires, opinons, evidence and arguments. And, as I stated at the beginning of this book, a primary driver for conversation amongst believers centers around Bigfoot mating habits and other louche theories.

What would a Bigfoot soiree look like? I will leave that to the imagination. I feel as some readers will not believe that a Bigfoot subculture exists.

Don't believe me? Here are very real topics, copied straight from forums and chat rooms. These are not made up or enhanced in any way.

Bigfoot Forum topics (some of these are dated):

1. "$1,000,000 bounty for Bigfoot—any takers?"
2. "Changing or desecrating Bigfoot formations—What happens if you urinate on one?"
3. "Is global warming forcing Bigfoot to head north?"
4. "Bigfoot birthing—wonder what it's like"
5. "The Giants of Okefenokee Swamp"
6. "Where has all the smell gone?"
7. "What are they doing with (Bigfoot) bones and the bodies?"
8. "Is the Eastern Bigfoot a Bigfoot/human hybrid?"
9. "Could Bigfoot be feral humans?"
10. "Baiting with women"

11. "Would a human and Bigfoot mating produce offspring?"
12. "Bigfoot mating—has anyone ever reported it, heard or seen it?"
13. "INFRASOUND and Bigfoot"
14. "Any evidence of polygamy in Sasquatch?"
15. "6 feet or 20 … How tall is your Bigfoot?"
16. "Bigfoot and *courting couples*—in parked cars etc."
17. "Interbreeding with a Bigfoot"
18. "Burned Bigfoot captured by government"
19. "Orangutan escape"
20. "Human or not—What's your take?"
21. "Bigfoot's Weenie—Why would he rip it out?"
22. "Lure Bigfoot with pornography—Could it work?"
23. "Clay County Bigfoot—My years of nightly visits"
24. "Could ants be a part of the Bigfoot diet?"
25. "Attracting Sasquatch with music"
26. "Best gun for Bigfoot?"
27. "Government holding evidence of Bigfoot—federal government hiding a Sasquatch body from public"
28. "Road Kill for Sasquatch—Bigfoot seeks out road kill"
29. Sasquatch, a multidimensional being—Could the legend himself be from another dimension?"
30. Research idea … spring sucker spawn!"

These are only a few of the very real topics on multiple forums. A sponsor's link on one of the Bigfoot forums said this (I am not joking--cross my heart, hope to die, stick a needle in my eye.)

MEET LOCAL HIKERS!

View Photo Profiles. Local Singles into Hiking. Join Now for Free.

Now, Bigfoot researchers can meet local, swinger hikers! What better way to score than to find a compatible female or male and walk off into a large and deserted forest? I mean, really, would you "meet up" with a single hiker for a "blind hike date"? If I'm a serial killer, I'm the first to sign up on the "Meet Local Hikers" website. And who would be more gullible than Bigfoot believers? If they are convinced that the spirit of the woods, the environment's guardian, the largest bipedal creature in the forest is there to protect them, why would they hesitate for a moment to accompany a stranger whom they met on the internet, for an intimate hike onto deserted trails?

Bigfoot believers get juiced on mythological fantasies. I wonder if it's emptiness in their lives (whether real or perceived) that compels them to look for meaning, to search for something greater than themselves, something superior to a real world that holds them back from achieving greatness. Or, is it true belief, that worm in the gut that tells you that an idea is true? What better way to think oneself superior than to own and nurture a unique awareness that common man could never comprehend? Like UFO abductees, they claim special knowledge of worlds beyond the normal, have in their possession a truth that separates them from the ignorant masses. The true believers who think that Bigfoot has one large size 25EEE in the physical world and the other 25EEE in the spiritual world are like the men and women who participate in Live-Action Role-playing (LARP). LARPers create fantasy worlds and kingdoms, build weapons such as maces, swords, and catapults; they cast spells and build cardboard fortresses to defend and attack—it's the Dungeons and Dragons crowd searching for meaning and control with those in disparate economic, psychological, and socio-economic circumstances. Similarities abound in these worlds. If one were to take a poll of LARPers who dress up as dragons, I'm willing to bet most believe in Bigfoot, UFOs, Merlin, Gandalf the White and inter-dimensional guardians. Some might even have sexual fantasies about Frodo. I'm also willing to bet people who participate wholly in LARPing and Bigfoot worship live in like neighborhoods, watch the same television programs, and generally work in related occupations. This is not a judgment. I know true believers and LARPers. I just don't understand the attraction to these games/belief systems/life views.

I also think that men who play fantasy football religiously and in multiple leagues would make perfect LARPers and true believers.

There are always exceptions. I know wealthy men who search for Bigfoot and otherwise grounded people who like to dress up as knights and joust. There are those who think an undiscovered North American ape might exist but are absolutely against any notion that Bigfoot appears and disappears at will, has magical powers, or uses telepathy to communicate.

Maybe most of the people who LARP, are Bigfoot true believers, or look forward to their next alien anal probe are in denial. The current of unhappiness resulting from spouses, occupations, living arrangements, children, etc. is rejected and then replaced by fantasy. *"I am happy here searching for the mystical Bigfoot, and I repressed my misery, so therefore this reality is acceptable. I am extraordinary."*

Am I the one in denial? If Bigfoot is real, don't I look the fool?

While others enjoy themselves with people of like minds, to include fun, excitement, Bigfoot singing, foam swords, stick-knocking, and sex with strangers, I joined the military, traveled the world, slogged through a government contractor career, started a company, sold the company, started another company and now think that I am somehow special enough to represent 740,000 people as a Congressman--which makes me part of a political subset of humans that feel compelled to look for meaning also, to search for something greater than themselves, something superior to a real world that holds them back from achieving greatness. I aspire one day to be successful through writing, and frolic though my own fantasy world as someone who thinks I hold relative importance, that my monogamous relationship is "normal," and that Bigfoot spirits, alien proctologists, and wizards are abnormal.

What if I'm wrong?

How is happiness defined? What is joy?

On or about 2009, my Queventelliur-loving former United States Marine Corps pal once came to my home to sup with my wife and three daughters. Despite his infatuation with the mystical Bigfoot, he was a fine fellow.

During our meal of chili and cornbread, my USMC brother related multiple stories of encounters with his floating hairy friend. Christine didn't flinch, her conditioning and tolerance at such high levels that tales of nighttime inter-dimensional hirsute travelers was as common as weather discussions between old men. I found myself enraptured by his stories, many involving prophecy, affirmations and warnings. He seemed happy and content. He explained that the Queventelliur communicated telepathically, always floating above him horizontally and looking down on him (My imagination conjured up some hellacious images)

Christine and I listened with an open-mind. All was copacetic until my USMC pal said, "I've been told there is an unhappy spirit in the house."

Christine stopped mid-chew.

I nodded. Solemn. "Where?" I asked.

"Your daughter's bedroom," said USMC pal. "I can get rid of it for you."

"Bigfoot told you this?" I asked.

"He did," said USMC pal. "Last night."

"Well," I said, spiking my napkin on the table like a tight-end spiking a football, "Let's go find that spirit."

Now, I can imagine what you, the reader, must be thinking. Shouldn't there be a challenge question? Maybe, "How the hell does mystical Bigfoot know this?" Or, something like, "Honey, did you spike the chili with LSD?" Or, maybe, "Hey USMC pal, please leave and take vaporous Chewbacca with you." Of course, there were no challenge questions. This, dear reader, was research. We were Bigfoot ghostbusters heading into an otherworldly transition zone.

I, my wife and three daughters followed USMC pal through the dining room and then up our stairs to the second floor. He stopped abruptly at the entrance of my youngest daughter's bedroom, reached for the latch and slowly pushed her door open. I was completely stunned at what I saw---her bed had been made! Was this unhappy spirit preternaturally tidy, despising the unholy clutter left by a precocious twelve-year-old? I quite liked this unhappy spirit.

"Don't turn on the light. The spirit is here," said USMC pal

Obviously, I thought. *It made her bed.*

USMC pal gestured for us to make a circle. We dared not speak as we interlocked hands and stood with slightly bowed heads. The room was 12'X12' so our circle of six almost completely filled the space next to the tidy bed. I so wanted to be dismissive of my USMC pal, to mock the whole proceeding as another bizarre Bigfoot ritual. But, I couldn't. USMC pal cared about our family and his noble, compassionate need to fix a spiritual rift in my home touched me in a way that's hard to qualify.

"It's ok," said USMC pal to the spirit. His voice softened to almost a whisper. "You're not in danger."

He beckoned the spirit to leave peacefully, to follow the light. He cajoled the spirit. He emboldened the spirit.

"GO to the light," USMC pal now demanded. "Leave in peace!"

Quiet. We stood. Hands locked. And then USMC pal breathed in deeply.

"It's gone," he said. I opened my eyes. Wife and daughters glanced about the room. A few moments passed.

My youngest daughter said, "It feels better in here now. Thank you."

USMC pal hugged her and each one of us.

What if I'm wrong about Bigfoot and those who believe blindly in Bigfoot's multiple manifestations? And, what if telepathic Bigfoots spoke in French?

It's a conundrum.

EATING AT THE BS BUFFET

Watoga State Park advertises itself as wilderness. During our first night searching for Bigfoot in the valley of the solitary bridge, I had assumed that the park had little human activity. Familiarity with the vastness of the Monongahela Forest and the few small towns bordering Watoga reinforced this assumption. I looked forward to the second day. I was not so much excited at the prospect of finding Bigfoot as simply wanting to enjoy a natural wilderness area. Watoga is just over 10,000 acres. Spinner and I awoke relatively late in the morning, around 08:00 a.m., due to the late night before. We ate a quick hot breakfast of bacon and eggs. I find the sizzle of bacon on a cook-stove to be one of life's great auditory pleasures.

The Riverside campground and its thirty-plus campsites teemed with Bigfoot searchers and few others. While we ate, a camp organizer approached Spinner and me and announced a get- together for all Bigfoot expedition participants at 10:00 a.m. That gave us time for clean-up and a quick shower. Not many of the participants spoke to one another during the trudges to and from the shower facilities. We simply grunted and waved.

At 10:00 the Bigfoot expedition participants gathered in

the center of the campground. The EL arrived in his rented SUV with a couple cabin residents. Don arrived in his minivan. (The EL, a few of the "special" guests, and Don stayed in climate-controlled cabins.)

"Today," said the EL, "we're to split up and find the best places for tonight's search. We'll explore each side of the river and look for possible Bigfoot habitat along trails and logging roads."

Despite my ambivalence about Bigfoot hunting, I expected a day filled with picturesque hiking and wildlife spotting. The weather was glorious, slightly overcast, temperature in the high sixties and little wind. With volume slightly above normal, the fast-flowing, green-colored river enthusiastically rolled over large rocks, creating miniature whitecaps and intimidating eddies.

Perfect day for wilderness exploration.

We split up into groups around noon. We wore light jackets. The temperature wasn't supposed to climb over sixty-five. Don's hip ached, so he elected to stay back and begin writing about his experience the night before.

Spinner and I accompanied two couples along a dirt road parallel to the Greenbrier River. The couples talked incessantly about their jobs, families, and other inconsequential trivia. Our irritation level increased exponentially in the first ten minutes. Spinner and I exchanged multiple looks and signals — raised eyebrows, smirks, slight head-shaking, rolling eyes, shrugs, shooting ourselves in the head with our pointer finger and sliding our thumbs across our throats. We also laughed at inappropriate times. We generally acted like assholes.

If they annoyed us too much, Spinner could shoot them.

"This road is well maintained," said Spinner.

I stared down its length. "There's a house down there."

One of the females, I'll call her Misty, said, "I see a few houses."

"There are lots of houses," said Spinner.

When we reached the first house in line, I jumped up on the porch and knocked. No answer. I tried opening the front door. It was locked. The residents kept the tidy rancher in immaculate condition. Wind chimes were free from rust. On the right side of the porch, a freshly painted double swing hung from sturdy eyehooks. The wooden planks had been recently treated with waterproofing. I walked around to the rear of the house. The recently fertilized green yard sloped gently to the river. The back door was also locked. This was not a park property that could be rented, but an honest-to-God residence.

And I was trespassing.

I also noticed trashcans on the side of the house.

"Nobody's here," I told the group when I rejoined them on the road. "Maybe the other houses are occupied."

"Let's check 'em out," said Spinner. I worry when he gets that gleam in his eye.

"Are you sure?" asked Misty. "I mean, could we get in trouble?" The other three grouped around Misty nodded their heads.

"Nobody's around," I said. "Who's gonna see us?"

Just then, all of us heard the coughing and sputtering of a vehicle engine. Across the river on the opposite hillside, a late eighties Ford truck pulled out of a rutted driveway connected to a dilapidated house. Smoke curled from the chimney.

"They might see us," said Spinner. He scratched his head. Spinner and I laughed.

The other four did not.

Spinner and I pressed on. The couples reluctantly followed. Their inane conversation stopped, and their mouths tightened. No more jocular ribbing. No more discussions about video games and Starbucks. For the couples, the hike had become a struggle for relevance. They realized that Spinner and I believed this Bigfoot thing to be preposterous and that we couldn't care less about their opinions or suggestions. Spinner and I now conversed freely, laughed about our "isolated location," discussed deer hunting and compared opinions about the previous Washington State expedition. The couples followed in sullen acceptance.

When Spinner and I reached the second house in line, our initial hypothesis was confirmed. Whether vacation homes or permanent residences, people occupied the houses along the river. A bicycle leaned against the siding. In the back yard, a child had scattered a few toys and left a ratty pair of play shoes used to wade in the river. Someone had recently dumped bags in the outside trashcans.

I stared back across the river and then turned around and studied the thickly treed mountainside on the other side of the well-maintained road. Even though houses lined the river, I wondered what we would see when we topped the peaks and descended into the wooly bush of the Monongahela. A theory crept into my mind. I shook my head to clear the theory. I could not accept that I was actually thinking seriously about Bigfoot, about why this stretch of the Greenbrier River might be a perfectly suitable place for Bigfoot to hang out. I did not believe in Bigfoot! Bigfoot is a meme! Bigfoot is a farce! Bigfoot is a money maker for charlatans! Bigfoot is a peyote-induced hallucination! Bigfoot is escapism!

"What's wrong?" asked Spinner. We had rejoined the couples on the well-maintained road.

"You know I don't believe in Bigfoot, right?"

"Yeah," said Spinner. He was suspicious. "I know."

Fitness is usually a prerequisite for hiking. The two pasty, doughy, and overweight couples were rapidly losing their enthusiasm, no doubt jonesing for half-pound hamburgers and milkshakes. Contributing to their despair might have been disappointment in realizing that humans occupied this section of Watoga State Park. Bigfoot probably wouldn't hoot and holler this close to multiple home sites, a campsite, and sputtering domestic trucks. Their growing dislike for me and Spinner wasn't helping their mood, either.

But now, I was going to give them a reason to hope.

Many Bigfoot researchers posit that Bigfoot is a Dumpster diver. Like bears, raccoons, and hobos, Bigfoot doesn't mind scooping leftovers from commercial or residential trashcans, especially if the Dumpsters border large tracts of uninhabited wilderness. Recently, a Florida man claimed to have staked out a strip-mall Dumpster for almost a month before coming face to face with a smelly skunk ape. His story follows:

Man recounts his meeting with Bigfoot

By GARY CORSAIR, DAILY SUN

In the early-morning blackness, partially bathed in a Hollywood-weird glow of incandescent light and

rolling fog, Dan Jackson slowly uncoiled from a half-hour crouch in his hiding place behind a garbage Dumpster.

What he saw — the very thing he had spent 20 years looking for — was so terrifying, Jackson would see it in his broken sleep for months.

A dark, hairy head. Glistening black eyes. A mouth full of bared teeth clenched in rage.

"He was huffing like a damn freight train," recalled Jackson, a venomous-snake expert from Lithia, who claims he came face to face with a fearsome creature he once didn't believe existed.

"In November 1983, if you had asked me whether I believed in Bigfoot or Sasquatch, I would have said, 'You mean that thing Hollywood made movies about? Are you crazy? No, of course not,'" says Jackson, an experienced outdoorsman who trapped alligators before he began extracting venom from snakes.

His opinion changed on a hog-hunting trip in a bay-head of sawgrass and cypress bog near Naples.

Jackson was tracking a "bunch of hogs" he had spooked when he became a believer.

"As I was looking into the sun, I saw a dark object about 150 yards away. I thought, 'Good, I'm going to have bear steaks tonight.' That's when what I thought was a bear, turned out wasn't a bear," Jackson recalls.

"It had been bending over, then it turned at the waist and looked at me. It had a black face and black eyes. It stood up and turned and walked on two legs right into the bayhead."

Jackson was momentarily paralyzed with fear.

"It scared me so bad, I forgot I had a shotgun in my hands. It wasn't a gorilla, and it wasn't a chimpanzee," Jackson said. "It was like water pouring into a computer. My mind just short circuited. What transpired might have taken 10 seconds. It could have been 10 hours for all I know."

When Jackson regained his senses, he investigated where the creature had crouched.

"Where his head came up to the cypress trees, I estimated it was 6 ½ to 7 feet tall," Jackson said. "The grass was matted down and there was a terrible smell. I equate it to someone who's been sleeping in a goat pen."

Back home, Jackson began spending long hours in libraries trying to learn all he could about what he saw. Even before the Internet was a household word, he found plenty of information.

"Everything I read indicated that it was peaceful, and never hurt a human," Jackson said. The more he read, the more he wanted to return to the Collier County bayhead.

"As often as I could, I went back down there. I wasn't trying to catch it or anything like that, it was just that I know I saw it, and I wanted to see it again."

Each time, Jackson tried something different. Night-vision goggles. Floating bait. Hiding in tree tops. He hung a tether ball off a tree limb in hopes of getting a handprint. He even mounted a mirror in the swamp, seven feet off the ground, because he had seen primates in a TV documentary lick mirrors. "Saliva contains DNA," Jackson reasoned.

"I admit, for the first two or three years it was probably comical the way I was doing things in the woods. But I started to get better and better. My techniques got better," Jackson said.

But he couldn't find what he calls the Florida Skunk Ape. Still, he was certain the creature was there, which made him only more determined.

"I can't look you in the eye and tell how I knew he was close, but I know there were times that he was," Jackson said. "I've been in the wild enough to know when something is wrong—times when it's like someone threw a switch and all the noise stops. You just knew that sucker was watching you."

Through years of searching, Jackson became convinced his prey was extremely clever.

"You're dealing with an intelligent creature, and he knows his environment better than you know your home," Jackson said. "I feel like he has a heightened sense of hearing, eyesight and smell. He knows you're there long before you know he's there."

If you believe Jackson on this point, then you'll probably believe his search encompassed 20 years.

"I'd go two to three times a month over a period of 20 years," Jackson said. "I was driven because I saw one of these things and I wanted to see it again."

Long after most people would have given up, he was finally rewarded.

"Eighteen years into my search, I found a footprint," Jackson said. "I found a group of smashed-down palmetto bushes, then a footprint, and then its next step was into a creek. It didn't come out on the other side. I would have seen where it came out because the other side was heavy brush. I went down the stream, but I didn't see any evidence where it left."

Jackson made a plaster cast of the 19 1/2-inch footprint, which he found "in the middle of the Everglades, 6.2 miles from the nearest road."

"I'm 6-foot, about 240. The impression my foot made where I found the footprint was barely a quarter-inch. Whatever made this track went down two inches," Jackson said. "You can't hoax this. Not where I found it. You'd put it where other people would find it."

An engineering professor Jackson estimated whatever made the footprint weighed "a little better than 500 pounds."

Jackson figured something that large must do some serious eating, so he began concentrating on what the Skunk Ape likely ate.

"I got smart and started watching game trails. I figured if I could find game trails, then I could find him," Jackson said.

Jackson hit the jackpot when a friend with thermal-imaging equipment took him for a nighttime helicopter ride over the area he had been searching. Jackson didn't see the Skunk Ape, but he saw the mother of all game trails.

The next night, Jackson began following the trail. After 21 days (during a six- to eight-week period) of meticulously "working the trail," he reached the edge of the woods. To his surprise, the trail ended near the rear of a new, small strip mall.

"At the back of the strip mall there were six brand-new Dumpsters," Jackson said. "I thought, 'Hot damn, I hit the jackpot. This where I am going to set up.'"

On the third night of his stakeout, he saw the Skunk Ape approach the dumpsters. Unfortunately, as Jackson moved from his hiding place at the edge of the woods, the creature ran away at a startling speed.

It was clear to Jackson that he couldn't sneak up on the creature. He would have to station himself closer to the Dumpsters.

Jackson stayed away for "eight or 10 days." During that time, he worked out a plan. He decided to put "bait" — a half-gallon of orange juice with sugar and chloral hydrate (triple the dose that would "drop a 250-pound man" he says) — in the Dumpster behind a pizza restaurant. He would place pop cans containing pebbles on the lids of the other Dumpsters, which would alert him to the arrival of the Bigfoot.

He considered setting up a video camera, but rejected the idea because of the "weird" lighting behind the strip mall. Plus, he knew his video would be dismissed as fake. If people questioned Roger Patterson's famous Bigfoot footage from 1967, they would surely dismiss anything Jackson produced.

At about 2 a.m. on the foggy night described in the opening paragraph of this article, Jackson, armed with a magnaported .44-Magnum in case the encounter turned violent, was crouched between two dumpsters when he heard a pebble-filled can hit the pavement.

"You've heard of the 'pucker factor'? Well, my 'pucker factor' went up," Jackson said. "Another couple cans hit the ground. Now my 'pucker factor' went up into the red zone. As I raised up, and brought my head above the top of the Dumpster, I saw a pair of eyes."

There was nothing friendly about the eyes just 10 feet away from Jackson's face.

"If he heard me, or smelled me, I don't know, but he had ahold of the Dumpster he was in and he was glaring at me with a look of rage on his face," Jackson said.

For the first time in his 20-year search for the Skunk Ape, Jackson feared for his life.

"My instinct was self-preservation. As I straightened up, he jumped out and landed; it was me and him. There's no way to describe the fear," Jackson said.

Jackson squeezed off a shot as the Skunk Ape leaped toward him; then, in a blink, it was gone.

"There's no way I would have been able to fire twice. He was gone that quick. He was tremendously fast," Jackson said. "It was one, two, three, and then it was over."

And so was his search. Forever.

"I had been lulled into a false sense of security. I always thought they were peaceful creatures. You didn't see the look in his eyes. It was purely a look of rage on its face," Jackson said. "I told myself, 'Dan, you idiot, you might get another chance. You saw his strength, don't push it.' Yeah, I had disturbed his supper, but it was more than that. What I'm going to tell you next, you're going to think I am crazy, but I think the rage was because I had outsmarted him."

Jackson created a stir in the Bigfoot research community when he posted his story on his Web site (Bigfoot, Skunk Ape & Me). Naturally, other seekers wanted to know where his frightening encounter took place.

"I have had requests from three who said they wanted to know the location and check it out. These people seemed too insincere and ill prepared, beside the fact that they were intending to spend only one night every other week to check things out," Jackson said. "Please excuse me here, but I worked on finding that location for a total of 21 days out of a month. It made me angry that they wanted to stand on my shoulders and try to do in one night what I had worked for and took the chances for so long to do. I've never told where it happened ... and I never will."

And Jackson, who is writing a book about his experience, remains adamant he is through searching for the Skunk Ape, Bigfoot, and Sasquatch— whatever you want to call it.

"I made the same mistake others had made; I wanted to prove it existed. And it almost cost me," Jackson said. "I'm satisfied. I'm not running into any lightning storms."[11]

I have serious misgivings about Dan Jackson's story. Was

---

11   Article was written by Gary Corsair, a senior writer with the Daily Sun. He can be reached at gary.corsair@thevillagesmedia.com.

the creature at the strip mall a large creature or a tiny Skunk Ape? If the creature was as large as the one in his previous sighting, how does Mr. Jackson miss a seven-foot, five-hundred-pound creature ten feet away with a magnaported .44-Magnum *while it was leaping toward him*? Was there enough light on a foggy night at 2:00 a.m. to observe the "rage on its face?" If he did hit the creature, was there a blood trail? Did the Bigfoot dimension-jump to escape injury? Why had no one else seen a Dumpster- diving Bigfoot? Does Bigfoot dodge bullets like Neo in the Matrix? Are there security cameras on the premises? How did he surmise that the Bigfoot was angry because he "outsmarted" it? How smart is a Dumpster-diving five-hundred-pound animal anyway? Why stop searching after establishing a standard operating procedure for finding Florida Skunk Apes? Did Dan call a latent fingerprint expert to lift Bigfoot "fingerprints" from the Dumpsters? Is the Patterson-Gimlin film controversy his real reason for not using a video camera? Did footprints lead away from the strip mall and did he cast them also? Why was he angry that others wanted to find the creature and only had a few days to spare— don't most people work for a living, hence their inability to search for *twenty-one days out of the month*? Wouldn't he want to share his knowledge at quite possibly the largest biological and zoological find in recent history? Lastly, why would someone whose occupation requires working with venomous snakes turn into a spineless sissy and swear off searching based on an encounter with what basically constitutes a large monkey?

Jackson's story is most likely fabricated.

And even though I don't believe this story, it reflects the

beliefs of many in the Bigfoot fraternity. Bigfoot is a hunter and a scavenger, is omnivorous, and is highly adaptable. He is the North American bipedal version of the African hyena.

So, as Spinner waited, and the doughy couples shuffled with impatience, I decided to share my theory. I spread my arms out, rotated my head left and then right, and said, "This whole river valley is a perfect trashcan buffet for Bigfoot. This is Bigfoot's winter food source."

The couples murmured to one another. Their eyes began to shine again. The sun glowed brighter. We now had a mission, an idea, a reason for inspecting the houses and the trashcans chained outside. Evidence of Bigfoot foraging might be found! We had a campfire story to tell. We could rationalize that the numerous sightings in and around Watoga State Park were proportional to Bigfoot's nutrition requirements.

My buffet bullshit inspired the couples. It even inspired me for an instant. The excitement of mental masturbation is contagious. I had formulated a theory based on numerous unsubstantiated claims, and it sounded magnificent! Even Spinner nodded with appreciation and respect. It is no small feat to fabricate such nonsense and to pronounce the nonsense with certainty. Jim Jones, David Koresh, and Charles Manson, the evil trio, must have experienced a similar emotion — electric warmth that spreads into the loins like sexual anticipation. Rapturous, addictive power; able to manipulate emotions and initiative for the malleable souls that believed…that wanted to believe.

It's hard to embrace skepticism for extended periods. It's just not fun. Truly, I wish for supernatural intervention during trying times in life. I crave something beyond the physical world. Spirits, bogeymen, Bigfoots, chupacabras, and guardian angels would make for a more interesting existence. The television show *X-Files* tapped into this wishful thinking, as Mulder and Scully searched for links between superficially unrelated paranormal phenomena.

Earth is one giant Petri dish for aliens.

Bigfoot raids trashcans for food and imparts wisdom to contactees.

Wouldn't that be cool?

The couples followed me and Spinner to a few more houses, where we observed trashcans. We searched for footprints along the edges of the roads, in muddy areas adjacent to the houses and yards inside the tree-lines bordering the yards. We discussed whether the latest rains would have washed the footprints away. We sniffed for Bigfoot musk. We giggled at the prospect of Bigfoot sneaking trashcan to trashcan, eyes glowing red, using his mental powers to mask his presence. The girls with us began to change, grow prettier. Their male friends became smarter, more engaging. We all drank from the Bigfoot spigot, an inebriation far surpassing vodka or tequila. We wore Bigfoot goggles. By combining empirical trashcan data with hypotheses about Bigfoot food- gathering during winter months, we surmised that Bigfoot could be more active during winter and harder to find in early spring. Searchers had to trek further into the wilderness, away from the homes along the Greenbrier.

We reached the end of the road. In front of us, the forest stretched into mountainous oblivion. For a second, I could imagine the possibility of a creature living undisturbed for millennia. Light-headed and in love with fantasy, I spread my arms wide and stated with baritone rapture: "Bigfoot lives here."

Then our family band radio crackled.

A voice said, "We have a sighting! Near camp!"

TWO BLACK THINGS

A quiet group greeted us. They waited. For her. The one who saw Bigfoot. Or *Bigfoots*.

Inside the Bigfoot Command Post (CP), the EL debriefed the eyewitness.

"She saw two of them," someone said while we waited for the official story. "On the trail along the river. It took her a couple hours to realize what she saw. It must have been a shock."

"When?" someone asked.

"Just after we started scouting," said another. "Bigfoot is so smart."

"Footprints?" asked someone.

A few people shrugged. No one had checked for footprints yet. Murmurs of expectation swelled like waves through the crowd.

Just as in the Washington State expedition, Spinner and I had missed a Bigfoot event. It seemed that Bigfoot sightings, rock throwing, weird howls, and spooky Bigfoot psychological attacks always happened when Spinner and I were not around.

Finally, the witness emerged from the CP.

"It's the Army guy's wife," said Spinner.

I didn't understand. Why would this kindly lady lie? Her husband provided the radios and equipment for the expedition. She had no corroborating witnesses, but she appeared honest.

The EL followed her out. She stood back as he waded into the crowd. We waited for his words.

"She saw two black figures walking beside the river," said the EL. "We need to find out if any of you were on the trail between 3:00 and 4:00 p.m." The EL pointed like Moses toward the river.

Everyone denied having been on the trail at that time. Every single expedition figure swore that they had been with others searching along both sides of the river bank. I glanced at the crew around us. No one wore black clothes, although from a distance, camouflage could be mistaken for black amongst shadows. Many wore camo. I wore a dark jacket. So did Spinner. We were the darkest of the bunch as far as clothing was concerned.

Her story went this way, more or less: After exiting her camper, she spotted two slender black figures at about 200 yards away. She grabbed her camera and walked to the river's edge, believing they were expedition members. When she arrived at the river bank, the two black figures mysteriously disappeared. She stared along the trail, down the river and up the steep hillside covered in mountain laurel. Where could they have gone? The only place to hide was in the mountain laurel and the nearly vertical jagged rock face of the river canyon that could not be climbed by a normal human. It was then that she acknowledged the oddities of the black things. She reported that they had lots of *space and daylight* between

153

their extremities, supporting her theory that they wore either light clothing or no clothing at all. They were "tree-trunk" dark. One of the creatures was tall, the other short.

"She saw two people," I said. "Simple. A tall person and a short person."

Spinner nodded.

A believer, overhearing my comment, said, with obvious disdain, "I don't think so. Lots of people hear and see weird things around here."

I didn't bother to argue. Neither did Spinner. We both were wrapped up in how a lady's description of two slender black things lazily tromping about on a well-marked and a non-surreptitious trail automatically translated to Bigfoot. She saw the two black things in daylight, early afternoon. Human activity was astoundingly high. Talking, clanging, and smelly humans had just walked both sides of the river only a half-hour before. Smoke from campfires still curled into the air. Had the creatures tiptoed around the humans, jumping from mountain laurel patch to mountain laurel patch before descending onto the trail *across from the campground where they were most likely to be spotted*?

Mountain laurel...the perfect hiding place for monsters. My grandfather would agree.

"This is crazy," I said.

Spinner nodded again. He was not his usual talkative self.

"I knew they were here," a believer said behind us. "I felt them all along."

I wondered where he *felt* them. Psychic communication? Infrasound? Floating above his sleeping bag?

A Bigfoot crew raced toward the purported sighting

location to search for footprints, scat, hair, baby Bigfoots, stick signs, rock piles, bent or snapped branches, and pungent odors. Already, the accepted explanation of two Bigfoots escaping up the hillside made its way from believer to believer. Like the telephone game, the stories became more incredible.

The Bigfoots were studying us!

It was a mother and child!

Maybe they were mates!

Something threw a rock at me this afternoon. Now I know what threw it!

Those are the ones that made the strange howls last night on the bridge!

The two black things morphed into substantiated Bigfoots within an hour. No longer did the believers in the group question whether the witness actually saw two black things, or if the two black things might be humans. Those two lanky black creatures represented all that was good and true in the world. It was a legitimized sighting, real honest-to-Queventelliur Bigfoots that scrambled up that impossibly steep hillside.

Barone sat with us during dinner, after the hubbub over the sighting dulled. We waved at those that walked by, but we didn't present ourselves as sociable—because we weren't sociable.

Barone broke the silence. "Think she saw Bigfoot?"

"Nope," I said.

"Spinner?"

"No, Don. Not a chance."

"Think she saw two black figures?"

"Nope," I said.

"No," said Spinner. "Not a chance."

"Think she's lying?" asked Don.

"Maybe," I said.

Don stared.

"She thought she saw two black things because she wanted to see," I said. "She's insane or caught in the mass psychosis around here."

"She's lying," said Spinner.

"She doesn't look like a liar," said Don. "I'm pretty good at spotting liars."

"I am, too," said Spinner.

Spinner dealt with drug dealers and criminals every day as a member of an elite counter-drug team. Don Barone is an accomplished investigative reporter. I'm pretty good at spotting a liar. All of us had participated in interrogations of some sort. Despite that, I had been duped before, as had Spinner and Don at one time or another. The woman's story about the creatures just didn't track. When I heard the story and the halting way in which it was told, my gut screamed *BULLSHIT!* I believed down deep that the woman either completely fabricated her story or sensationalized it after the fact. Proving deception was impossible, however. What if she simply imagined the whole event? Or what if two regular humans had been walking the trail and she simply took too much time to walk a few hundred yards?

How the people swarmed to her, congratulated her, praised her. This expedition had now become an unqualified success. Once again, the EL could report that Bigfoot lived in the wilderness. People saw Bigfoot or heard Bigfoot or *experienced* Bigfoot on every single expedition.

Weird stuff happens in the dark, and most of that weird stuff is attributable to Bigfoot. And, for only a small fee, you too can see, hear, and experience Bigfoot in the wild.

"You know what this reminds me of?" I asked Spinner.

Spinner shook his head.

"The lady in Washington who said she saw Bigfoot."

"Oh, yeah," said Spinner. He addressed Don. "Hours after we left, she swore that an eight-foot Bigfoot had walked toward us. At the time, she said she couldn't tell what it was. We were pissed. We were defenseless down there." Spinner's voice became louder. "I asked her why she didn't say something immediately, especially with seven other people around. She couldn't answer."

"Christine was with the lady," I said. "Christine didn't see a thing."

"You think people are too shocked to speak out?" asked Don. "Maybe they can't process what they're seeing."

"Possible," I said. "But I have another theory."

"Great," said Spinner.

"The Martha Effect," I said.

"Ah," said Spinner. "I forgot about that."

"I think people fool themselves into thinking they see things just to fit in with others. Almost a religious thing. Someone says, 'I talk to Jesus' and everyone flocks to the prophet. The prophet is bestowed with gifts like attention, popularity, credibility. Eventually, someone covets the prophet's status and says with holy fervor, 'I saw Jesus too!' They become a prophet...or at least an apostle. She might be lying. But I think she wants to be included in the Bigfoot inner circle. Therefore, one sees what they want to see."

"Why call it the Martha Effect?" asked Don.

"Because of Martha in Washington," I said. "She reported a Bigfoot twenty-four hours after she claimed to see one. Our theory started with her."

"Everyone is seeing things?" asked Don.

"Yes, that's what I believe," I said. "Maybe they're straight up lying or have misidentified an animal in the woods. Simple pimple."

"Hallucinations," suggested Don.

"Absolutely," I said. "Sleep paralysis, alcohol- or drug-induced, or maybe sleep deprivation. All the usual suspects. Or insanity. I think crazy people are attracted to Bigfoot, too. They don't come right out and yell, 'Hey, I'm nuts!' They're like functioning alcoholics. A functioning alcoholic can drink all day and still work in a profession and interact with non-alcoholics damn close to normally. A functioning true believer can do the same thing. They could be conversing in hoots and whistles with Bigfoot in their dream-world while operating heavy machinery or managing mutual funds."

AN HONEST MAN?

Déjà vu is an odd and alternately comforting and disturbing sensation that ripples through the conscious mind like an incoming tide. *I've been here before*, it tells you. Whether in a past life or idealized from a repressed or cloudy memory, *I'm telling you* that *you've been here*.

Since I don't believe in past lives, a pesky repressed or cloudy memory must have been invading my brain, when the airline pilot said over the intercom, "To your left you can see Mount Rainer...and just beyond Mount Rainer you should be able to see Mount St. Helens."

Almost four years had passed since I last flew into Seattle. This time I was alone. Four years ago, I sat in an aisle seat, my wife sat in the middle and Spinner sat by the window. Now, I sat in an aisle seat, the middle seat was empty, and a stranger with the remains of a recently popped zit on her nose stared out the window. I missed that time long ago, when Spinner, Christine, and I whispered excitedly about our adventure camping trip disguised as a Bigfoot expedition. I missed those heady moments, those virginal expectations of orgasmic discovery. Even though I was skeptical then, I expected a well-organized event, a cavalcade of expert testimony, arduous hikes, and passionate investigation.

Instead I got an education.

"To your left you can see Mount Rainer…and just beyond Mount Rainer you should be able to see Mount Saint Helens." I was quite sure that the airplane pilot from that initial Bigfoot expedition had uttered those exact words. I looked across the aisle and out the opposite window. *Déjà vu*. Snow-capped Rainer and drab Saint Helens right where the pilot said they would be. I wondered as we banked toward the tarmac if Bigfoot, either the Bigfoot of Missing Link or Extraterrestrial or Harmonic Universe or Great Spirit origin, stared at the big silver birds in the sky.

I was here on official government business for the National Security Agency. My meetings started the following day, Wednesday.

But today, August 26th, 2008, I was here to see Bob Gimlin.

The most famous Bigfoot film and definitive proof for Bigfoot believers is the the P-G film. Roger Patterson and Bob Gimlin captured the footage in the early afternoon on October 20, 1967. For sixty seconds, a hairy "female" creature strode effortlessly along the sandy banks of Bluff Creek. Roger Patterson captured the creature on his sixteen-millimeter Kodak hand-held camera. Bob Gimlin stood at the ready with his 30-06. Frame 352 is the most famous frame of all. It shows "Patty," the female Bigfoot, glancing over her shoulder at the two hairless humans.

The P-G film is considered ultimate proof of Bigfoot's existence to Bigfoot believers. Believers routinely state that experts have validated its authenticity.

The P-G film is considered one of the world's greatest hoaxes by an army of skeptics. Skeptics state that experts have proven it's hogwash.

As my friend in the Air Force used to say: "We have a conundrum here."

I drove from Seattle to Union Gap, Washington. Mel, my Native American pal, was meeting me and Bob at a restaurant called Shari's. In my rented Mitsubishi, I drove through Issaquah, zipped over the Snoqualmie Pass, and whipped past Ellensburg. Mel had investigated Bigfoot sightings in Ellensburg. Apparently, Bigfoot visited the orchards bordering the south side of the interstate. As I drove by, I stared at those twisted orchards and wondered what a Bigfoot would look like as it munched on a juicy apple.

I arrived in Union Gap at 4:32 p.m. Even though I had met Bob before, I felt strangely expectant, like today would somehow highlight either the extraordinary possibilities of Bigfoot's existence or prove beyond a doubt that Bigfoot was simply a long-running hoax, perpetrated by money-hungry con men hoping to make a quick buck by taking advantage of society's less-rational souls.

I pulled into the restaurant parking lot. Under the Shari's sign, I saw Bob Gimlin sitting in his older-model SUV. I knew it was Bob, because I recognized his off-white cowboy hat. It had been four years since we talked face-to-face. I parked two spaces from him. I inhaled deeply. I exhaled. I exited the vehicle just as he climbed from his.

Bob was in surprisingly good shape for a man of seventy-eight years. He almost loped when he walked, even though I noticed a slight limp on that day. His wiry frame was devoid of cellulite, his waist measured at most thirty inches. He didn't weigh a pound over one hundred fifty. A horse trainer by trade, he outworked and outrode men half his age. When he shook your hand, he stared you in the eyes, ascertaining your worth as a man. In return, his piercingly blue, clear, and alert eyes hid nothing. Instead of detracting from his face, his deep, weathered wrinkles added a certain depth, a kindly homage to a physically demanding existence. His dungarees were well-worn, not the pre-washed vanity variety sold at Hollister's or Abercrombie and Fitch, but snug-fitting functional Wranglers that belonged to a working man. He was not the John Travolta of the mechanical bull in *Urban Cowboy*. Bob was the quintessential working horseman, a man who worked alone but was not alone. He kept friends for life and was a devoted husband to his protective wife Judy.

"It's good to see you," said Bob. His voice was baritone played through fine gravel. Rumor had it that Bob's voice was to women like a snake charmer's pungi[12] was to snakes.

I shook his hand and patted his shoulder. "You haven't changed a bit."

"Mel coming?"

"About a half hour or so," I said. "I just talked to him on the cell phone."

"I haven't seen Mel in a month."

We walked into Shari's restaurant. All the waitresses were well-fed but not obese, kind in speech, and attractive in a matronly way. Our server led us to a spiffy table by the window. I opened the menu. This was American food, the quintessential smorgasbord of hamburgers, meat dishes,

---

12   A pungi is the snake charmer's instrument. It consists of two reeds or bamboo tubes. One is for the melody and the other is for the drone. These are attached to a larger cavity made of gourd. The pungi can be played for its interesting sounds or used as a decorative item and conversation piece.

fried chicken, and fried fish. I chose a prime rib sandwich au jus, most commonly known as a French Dip. Bob had eaten earlier. He ordered coffee. He kept his hat on.

Bob and I discussed his bum knee, his wife, and his horses, and then I finally managed to ask him something I never asked him before.

"I know a thousand people ask to you about Roger Patterson and the P-G film," I said. "But, after all these years do you think you could have been hoaxed?"

Bob removed his glasses, sat them by the salt shaker at the corner of the table, and began to talk.

"I didn't believe in Bigfoot at first. Just didn't have time for it. Roger wouldn't leave me alone about Bigfoot. He made me listen to cassettes of people who saw Bigfoot. He asked me to go on searches with him. I couldn't afford to go with him on these searches, but I finally went on one because Al DeAtley paid for it. I was hot-roofing then. I had to work for a living, so I asked my boss for a few weeks off. My boss didn't like it, but he agreed to lay me off for a while."

Who's Al DeAtley?" I asked

"He was the man financing the Bigfoot trips. Al was Roger's brother-in-law. He owns Superior Asphalt, has the biggest house in the county."

At the time of our discussion, Al DeAtley was still alive and a stalwart in the Yakama County community. Bob did mention that at the time of the Bigfoot film, on or about October 20, 1967, Superior Asphalt was not doing well.

Bob continued. "Well, when we went to Bluff Creek there were footprints everywhere. Roger was excited. I still wasn't quite sure what to make of these creatures." (It should be noted that Roger Patterson suffered from lymphoma and was rumored to be destitute—hence his need for investors like Al DeAtley). "So, we looked for the creature where it had been seen and where we found footprints. We saw it and filmed it."

I did not ask him about the sighting specifically. Four years earlier, I listened as he told his encounter to Bigfoot enthusiasts. I had read his account. I was familiar with the many opinions and studies related to Roger and Bob's sighting, and I had enough background to formulate my own ideas on whether the circumstances surrounding the film were suspicious. Of course, Bob knew, as did Mel who had joined us by this time, that I am a Bigfoot skeptic. I believe the Patterson-Gimlin film is a hoax.

But who hoaxed it?

I've read as many P-G film analyses as I can stand: Grover Krantz, David Daegling, Greg Long, Dmitri Donskoy, etc. Conspiracy theories abound, and scientific evidence proves the authors' belief systems on both sides in every respect. If one believes in Bigfoot, the P-G film corroborates that belief. If one does not believe, the P-G film and the circumstances surrounding the film (including the money trail and the preponderance of hoaxes and carnival sideshows in the 1960s) prove that the P-G film was a hoax. My questions to Bob pertained to the personal strain that the film had caused him and his wife, as well as how Bob reacted to the almost supernaturally absurd theories on the film itself. In some instances, believers suggest that Bob Gimlin, Roger Patterson, and an unknown third member of the party (Bob Heironimus, Al DeAtley or some other conspirator) killed a whole family of Bigfoots and that Patty was the hairy mama come back to mourn. So, it was a legitimate film AND a conspiracy AND a murder AND a cover-up.

A real spine-tingler!

I asked again, "Could you have been hoaxed? Your reputation as a stand-up guy would give the film credibility."

Bob nodded and sipped his coffee. "Anything's possible. Awfully hard to make a Bigfoot suit, though."

I asked, "How about those who wrote about you? What do you think of them?"

"Greg Long[13] tried to come in my house, actually put his foot in the door. My wife told him to back off or he would be sorry. A lot of these people are crazy. They want to find something that isn't there."

I agreed that they acted crazy. But I did not mention that the circumstances leading up to the making of the P-G film would make any freethinking skeptic suspicious.

Bob continued. "And I can't believe they think I shot Bigfoot and buried it up there."

"Who thinks that?"

"M.K. Davis," said Bob.

"Wow," I said.

"He did a film study where they steadied the film up. Took the shake out of it. Says he can spot where we buried the thing. Even sees blood and backhoe tracks. I explained to them how hard it would be to do that. Impossible." Bob

---

13   Greg Long wrote "The Making of Bigfoot." He claims that Phillip Morris constructed the Bigfoot suit and that Bob Heironimus was the man who wore the suit. Although not a huge fan of Long's writing style or techniques in recreating the mood and tenor of 1967, I am impressed with his tenacity in tracking men and women involved with Roger Patterson and his business ventures. Greg Long concludes that Bob Gimlin was a willing conspirator in the Patterson-Gimlin Bigfoot film hoax.

fiddled with his coffee mug handle. "Nobody took a shot up there."

"How many theories are there, Bob?"

Bob smiled. "Too many. A long time ago, I swore I would ignore them. Judy and I have been through hell. She stood by me for forty-five years."

"Good woman," I said.

I thought of my own wife. She would do the same. I could tell the world that I saw a cross-eyed leprechaun riding a Tyrannosaurus Rex, and she would swear on a stack of Bibles that I told the truth. She might even say, "The leprechaun gave us the finger. Mean little sucker."

"You know, I don't do this stuff to find the creature," said Bob. "I just tell people what I saw. If they believe me, that's fine. If they don't believe, that's fine too. I don't even care so much about all of this. But I can't ask for better friends. They're worth more to me than Bigfoot."

"What about these organizations that look for Bigfoot?"

"They might do *some* good," said Bob. "But you don't need an organization to look for Bigfoot. People tell me all the time that they must ask permission from this person or that to go searching for Bigfoot. That's a bunch of bull. Anyone who can go in the woods, write down what they saw, and share it with everyone is just fine. As long as you're smart about it and tell the truth, that's as good as anything else."

"A lot of money out there," I said.

"No one owns Bigfoot," said Bob. "And I've never taken any money for the film. I went to court once and we couldn't agree on what my share was. So I walked away."

Everything in me screamed to ask him the one question I

knew most would want to know: *How much did you walk away with?* But I didn't. I wanted to ask him about Al DeAtley, Rene Dahinden, Peter Byrne, and Grover Krantz. I didn't do that, either. My reasons are simple--true believers and skeptics could conclude that I am part of some sordid multigenerational cover-up. My book is not meant to expose a hoax. It is not meant to prove or disprove Bigfoot specifically. My book is about Bigfoot mythology. It is about the current crop of Bigfoot money managers and those who believe completely in the Bigfoot phenomenon. Bob Gimlin is the embodiment of that belief system. A hoax can never be proven unless Bob Gimlin confesses, or Al DeAtley and any number of those involved with the actual planning and execution of a hoax come forward. Furthermore, the P-G film is a self-licking ice cream cone. The film's impact, or *infection* if you will, spread like an airborne virus. Even if the film is proven a hoax to within a whisker of one hundred percent, true believers will simply say, "It doesn't matter. Bigfoot is true in my heart. Bigfoot sustains me. Bigfoot created my persona. Because of Bigfoot I have friends. Because of Bigfoot I have a spouse. Because of Bigfoot I have a life. Because of Bigfoot I am blessed. Because of Bigfoot, I transcend mediocrity and the humans that populate that pedestrian realm. Because of Bigfoot I get laid. I am special."

I admire Bob's backbone. Roger Patterson left Bob in an untenable position. When Roger died, all questions about the creature, the hoax, and those involved fell on Bob's narrow shoulders. If it is true that Roger and Bob alone filmed Patty on that day in 1967, then Bob is the last remaining witness to an extraordinary biological event. If Roger perpetrated a hoax without Bob's knowledge, Bob should remain consistent in recounting his version of events. Bob could suspect Roger in a hoax, but Bob cannot—will not—throw Roger under the bus. Some might argue that Bob protects Roger because of Bob's complicity in the hoax, and that money changed hands that guaranteed silence for the rest of their natural lives. Possibly. I'll confess that if my closest friend and I hoaxed the world, I would never admit to the hoax, money or no money, especially if my closest friend died and left a family behind.

Bob Gimlin held his ground.

He continued. "I got a phone call from a friend of mine one night. He was real angry. He told me that a man claiming to be me was with Roger Patterson and Al DeAtley at a Bigfoot movie showing. I couldn't believe it. My friend stood up and said, 'You're not Bob Gimlin. Who the fuck are you?' My buddy was thrown out of the place. He also told me that there were hatfuls of cash beside the entrance. That made me angry."

"Are you still angry?" I asked.

"No. Roger apologized to me on his deathbed. He said he shouldn't have done that. I forgave him. He looked real bad."

Silence. I tried to imagine the scene. Roger lay dying and apologized for his bad deed. What was Bob to do then? By 1972, when Roger died, tension between Roger and Bob had increased, as the film became more of a financial flashpoint and the object of increased scrutiny.

Our conversation turned mundane for a while. We talked of Bob's horses, building fences, the differences in work ethic between generations (we all agreed that men were tougher in the past), Mel's work as a forester on the Yakama reservation, and my book. I told Bob and Mel that my book investigated those who believed in all the different versions of Bigfoot. I explained that some people believed Bigfoot to be an inter-dimensional guardian or a seed race of extra-terrestrials. This made Bob and Mel laugh out loud.

"Bigfoot isn't a spirit or some kind of extraterrestrial--it's an ape or something," said Bob.

"Yes, that's true," said Mel.

"You know," said Bob, "Judy was worried about me talking to you. But I told her you were one of the good guys."

His statement surprised me. "I think I am. If you remember, the first time we talked, I didn't ask you about the film. Christine wanted to talk about horses. I left you and my wife alone for hours."

"I thought that was nice," said Bob.

"I figured you get tired talking about the film all the time. It must be hard being the most important man in Bigfoot research." I smiled.

He smiled back and sipped his coffee.

"Okay, I have to ask this." I took a deep breath. "What about Bob Heironimus?" Bob Heironimus claimed to be the man in the Bigfoot suit.

After a chuckle, Bob Gimlin said, "Bob wasn't a rocket scientist. He was just a good old boy who got caught up in it. I liked Bob. He was a big strong man. I don't think Bob wore a Bigfoot suit, though."

Before I could ask another question, Bob added something that perplexed me.

"The creature didn't look like the film, "said Bob. "It was different."

"How so?" I asked.

"Hard to explain, but the creature looked different than it did on film."

"Did you ever go back to the spot?"

"I did, many years later. But I couldn't find the exact location. I wish I would have returned immediately after we saw it, but there was so much going on...." Bob trailed off. He must have suspected that I had read about and researched the timeline after the sighting. Bob's behavior after the incident is questioned by many. Instead of celebrating with Roger and Al over the incredible good fortune of filming Bigfoot, Bob went home and slept. Bob explains that he was exhausted from his considerable efforts in extricating his truck and horses from the Bluff Creek area during awful storms. He told me as much during our conversation. Just like with the story of his alleged murder of the Bigfoot family, Bob scoffed at the notion that he immediately tried to separate himself from Roger and Al DeAtley, that his absence suggested a feeling of guilt or fear on his part.

"I was just tired," said Bob. "Real tired. Even with this backhoe story that M.K. Davis came up with...I didn't use a backhoe to bury Bigfoot bodies. I would have had to get heavy equipment in there after the fact. I didn't sleep for almost three days.

"Listen," said Bob. "My father taught me that if you borrowed a nickel from someone, you would drive one hundred miles just to pay that nickel back. He also taught me that if someone borrowed a nickel from you, you get that nickel back, even if that means making them pay you back. I was taught honesty. I was taught to be tough. You have to be a man."

I finished my sandwich. Mel and Bob talked. The sun was setting. Tomorrow, I would visit the Boeing facility in Seattle on official business.

"Want to hear a joke?" asked Bob.

"Sure," I said.

"What's the difference between a fairy tale and a cowboy's story?"

"I don't know, Bob." I smiled in anticipation of the punch line.

Bob lifted his coffee mug up and smiled. "A fairy tale starts with *Once Upon a Time*...a cowboy's story starts with *No shit, wait until you hear this.*"

BIGFOOT THE ROCK STAR

So here I am. 2020. I finished most of the final draft in 2017. Hard to believe that I waited to finish this book. For years I sat on the fence, hoping that those claiming to be true believers (for money's sake) would be exposed. I waited. And lived. And waited. I started and sold analysis and technology companies, built a distillery, even thought about building a brewery that served only Italian beer and wood-fired pizza. I'm fifty years old now. My grandfather died not too long ago. He was eighty-one. And the story of the Mighty Peculiar died with him. Maybe that was the spark that pushed me to finish this book about the various sects of Bigfoot believers. Maybe I'm still angry about the crap released by my political opponent and her"Bigfoot Erotica" nonsense. Maybe I'm flabbergasted and amused by the Bigfoot tripe on television. Maybe I'm done humoring the multitude of conspiracy theorists that hide in plain sight.

Shows like *Finding Bigfoot*, *Killing Bigfoot*, *Mountain Monsters*, and *Survival Man--Bigfoot* infest our televisions and computers. Bigfoot hokum shows are outlandish, ridiculous, and inane in their theories and pronouncements. These shows are entertainment only. I just can't imagine that Bigfoot media types convinced televison network personnel that natural forest sounds (whether in California or Bangladesh), wood knocks, unproven guttural noises, flashing lights and coyote yips are somehow nine-foot-tall monsters that have eluded science, infrared cameras, thermal imagery and auto collisions. The networks must know without a doubt that the shows are fake, and that viewers will watch out of true belief or to waste time on fantastical shows dripping with pseudo-scientific psychobabble. I am amazed as I watch the hands of *Finding Bigfoot* audience members shoot up when asked if they have, indeed, witnessed these hirsute phenomena. It is possible that many have seen a hairy beast of some sort, but I believe that some that raise their hands are glory hounds, wanting so badly to be singled out on a fringe nature channel show. Afterwards, while drinking beer and moonshine beside a campfire, these glory hounds regale their peers about pulling the "wool over the eyes" of stupid-ass television people. Those stories would create a kind of backwoods fame for said charlatans.

Then I wonder to myself--would my grandfather have been one of the crazies? Doubt pushes into my soul--the *WELL, MAYBE* thought that all of us have from time to time—*well, maybe* UFOs exist. *Well, maybe* this condom under my bed isn't from my wife's lover. *Well, maybe* wood fairies dance in the meadows. *Well, maybe* Garcinia Cambogia will help me lose one hundred pounds this month. *Well, maybe* Bigfoot is out there.

I have hunted, fished and hiked in forests around the United States and in foreign countries more times than I can count. I have been isolated and in the dark. Nothing like a Bigfoot-- biological, interstellar, interdimensional or otherwise--has ever snuck, teleported, appeared or manifested his large, camouflaged backside into my camp. No monsters. I've seen bears. I've seen elk. I've seen deer. I've seen all manner of wildlife, from the furtive bobcat to a porcupine. While watching these television shows--I watch these shows because I have researched this topic extensively--I have yet to see a Bigfoot. And yet, people keep watching and believing. Bigfoot is not a faith-based entity to most of us (he is an inter-dimensional being to some), but I must conclude that most Bigfoot devotees believe because of, well, maybe … faith.

When running for elected office here in the great Commonwealth of Virginia, I experienced a familiar feeling of curious dread while listening to activists on the far right and the far left. Some were alight with a belief so sure that no earthly logic could shake it, like those Bigfoot believers I encountered, whether BE, GA, MM or Interstellar. I have a healthy skepticism for the actual beliefs of those who shill for money for political reasons or those who shill from past Bigfoot expeditioners like me (I think most of the emotion is fake), and I've peered into the glowing eyes of the most convicted true believers, those desperate souls who believe in Bigfoot. I have witnessed that same unearthly glow in the eyes of anarcho-marxist political activists and QAnon conspiracy theorists. The glow frightens me. That glow means that the mental elevator might be stuck between floors. That glow means these people will fight for the irrational and against the rational, no matter the stakes.

Extended, expert observation of creatures, and people, in their natural habitat is the only way to ascertain what is true and what is not true. In this crazy world of ours, rational thought is in short supply. It's at the bewildering intersection of mythology, pseudo-science, social media, profit and camping cum dating that searching for the ever elusive Bigfoot can become...complicated.

BIGFOOT EXTERMINATORS INC. (EXCERPT).

The Partially Cautionary, Mostly True Tale of Monster Hunt 2006

by DON BARONE AND DENVER RIGGLEMAN

"If you can't control your fear, you can't control nothing."

--My dentist…
but it also applies
to monster-hunting

Dateline: N 43° 42′ 35″ W 73° 56′ 11″ Elev: 1131 1:05 am EST

Everything is green.

Gen-3 night-vision green. Night vision so powerful, a firefly becomes Mothra-like.

When the bug's rear end light goes on, the flash temporarily blinds you.

An up-to-no-good green.

The forest to my left, with an open meadow beyond, all bathed in fluorescent green. An empty drainage ditch to my right, same

175

freakin' green. An area that Bigfoot Hunter/possible DOD spy guy Denver called "a perfect Sasquatch freeway."

"They'll come right down this track here," he said.

And "here" is exactly where I'm standing. On a Blair Witchy green abandoned railroad track. All alone.

Tonight, I'm a Bigfoot roadblock.

I'm 50 yards behind the Bigfoot Hunters, and they have guns. I have a plastic telescopic Wal-Mart hiking pole for protection.

And something just howled in my right ear.

And no one else heard it. But me. Me and my adjustable stick.

"Denver...Spinner...ah, little help, dudes." I know I said it, but I never heard the words. I did hear a beep, then two beeps, and then three.

On the fourth beep, the super-duper sort-of-borrowed-from-a-state-police-fugitive-squad- team Gen-3 night vision went out.

Darkness sweeps in, so thick, so black, the only thing visible is fear.

That's when the howl begins in my left ear. On the Sasquatch Superhighway. The only movement is my walking stick thing, shaking.

Then I see my son, Jimmy, break off from the group and run back my way, straight into the howls.

"No, you are not getting my son!" I lift up my $3.99 Wal-Mart walking stick, and in a flash (that flash being about 2-3 seconds, being that I'm fifty-four and all), I spin to battle the beast...now with only half a walking stick since the bottom half—the one with the point I need—is left sticking in the mud. Great.

But I swing it nonetheless, like a madman at a Nordstrom half-price shoe sale, arms moving up, down, sideways. I let loose a close-in thrusting move I saw while lying on the couch watching Zorro, hoping that if the beast has private parts somewhere, wherever mythic beasts keep them, my half walking stick/sword will strike Bigfoot Balls.

At this point, I feel the tug. From my waist area, from damn near too close to my own mythic private parts. And that's when I see the iPod get ripped off my comfort-waist accommodating belt and fly off into the forest.

Flung there by my not-quite-Zorro-like walking-stick jab.

Arching into the 6 million-acre Adirondack National Park goes the brand new iPod belonging to Chris, my daughter Ashley's boyfriend...and as it bounces off the first pine tree, I hear the howls again, coming from the very expensive, extremely way too light earphones.

Earphones I forgot I had on.

Chris's iPod bounces off the tree stump in some physics-defying feat that will end up costing me several bucks and several minutes of tongue-lashing by Ashley, heading on a flight pattern straight for a God-knows-why preserved wetland.

On the second skip across the water, the howls go away, and the band, Deep Purple, starts singing, "Hush...hush...I thought I heard her name...glug, glug, glug."

My son Jimmy, listed as 6'4" in the HS Basketball program, 6'2" in the shower, is staring over my head, mouth open, eyes snapping between me and the general direction of the underwater guitar riff now playing for the frogs.

He says, "Huh...what the hell...Chris's new...Ashley's going to be pissed... Mom bought that for his Christmas gift...Jesus, Sad, you could have just erased the song...I'm not going in there... Denver.... brand new...what are you going to say.... swamp shit."

Thus begins my hunt for Bigfoot. Monster Tour: 2006.

With Deep Purple's dog-howling opening of "Hush" playing through ultra-light, forgotten earplugs in my ears.

And a little puddle of pee left on a darkened Bigfoot Boulevard.

Basecamp: N 43° 39′ 42″ W 73° 53′ 56″

Normally I just go to the beach. But not this summer.

This summer, I was somehow talked out of my annual looking at bikinis while pretending to read, and into looking for Bigfoot.

Instead of SPF-300-something, Spinner – Denver's undercover state cop friend, who even carries a throwaway piece on Bigfoot Hunts – is handing me some awful smelling "non-odor" especially made "for hunting things that can smell us"--100% DEET lotion.

Decked in full camo, he pushes the bug-killing spray bottle across the porch railing with one of his three carbon-blade hunting knives, and staring down at my dry-cleaned, very nicely creased Orvis cargo shorts with ducks on them, he runs his tongue between his front teeth and lip and mumbles to me, "You better put this on; the bugs will crawl up your ass before you know it."

Not wanting to have insects camping in my crack, I overlook the red 100% DEET warning label, knowing that my children are as deformed as they ever will be, and I spray it on my face.

"Might not want to do that," says Spinner, while pulling a Glock from his waterproof, minus-30-degree surviving hunting boots. He sights it on the Mickey Mouse ears I have stuck on my minivan's antenna.

I would have said something, but right at that moment both my lips and tongue were all tingly and numb-like from the 100% DEET oil covering my face. I'm thinking, bugs in the ass, not so bad after all.

We're in Riparius, NY, in mid-July, in a ski chalet that I booked over the internet, sight unseen, from some guy in Jersey. I'm in charge of the camping arrangements and rounding up the Bigfoot Inc. alleged experts, including the small town non-cell-phone-having weekly newspaper guy who believes Bigfoot and UFO's are somehow connected. I've also set up the interviews with two hunters and one PhD environmental biologist – all of whom have seen Bigfoot walking nearby.

Denver is the DOD (Department of Defense, for those of you living in the blue states) mission planner with an SUV filled with topographic and satellite maps borrowed from places we can't ask about. Denver is a lifelong hunter of deer, bear, and Commies, who, as a child with his grandfather, had a sighting of something "mighty peculiar" that keeps him on the quest for Bigfoot answers.

Denver told me he is writing a book about Sasquatch and soldiers. He also said he once beat the hell out of our camp-mate, Spinner, who said something about Denver's wife, Christine, having a "hairy back" when they both were in the Air Force together.

Spinner is our brush-cut weapons guy and resident skeptic. He's the camp cook, specializing in grease and barbecue. A Gulf War Vet, he told me over a piece of fried charred meat, "I think you'll find out it was me that beat the hell out of Denver when we first met."

Chris is my daughter's boyfriend that my wife, Barb, says we really like a lot. He's in MIS (Management Information Systems, for those of you lucky enough not to have to know that), a computer geek who always fixes all the bad things I do to my computer, when he and Ashley stop by for their weekly raid on our refrigerator. He used to have a kick-ass iPod. He has heard both Denver and Spinner mention my daughter Ashley and shotgun in the same sentence several times now around the campfire.

Jimmy, my teenage son and CT all-state/all-star volleyball player, has, including today, now spent one day in the woods in his entire life. He's the only one in the cabin who can figure out how to get the satellite TV to work and has beat Spinner three out of four times in the PS2 MLB game he brought with him.

Since I'm in charge of roughing it, we are doing without A/C in our cedar log A-frame cabin. Satellite TV, Pier-1 dish-stocked, granite countertop, brushed chrome kitchen appliances, three different kinds of donuts, and a Starbucks Caffè Verona brewing machine takes the edge off the humidity in Base Camp.

Just beyond our wrap-around porch lurks the Adirondack Forest of upstate NY. Six million acres — 9,300 square miles — where the nineteen people per square mile who live here are way out numbered by deer. More bears than pickup trucks.

And Bigfoot. We're told.

MISSION PLANNING

There's nothing like waking up to the sound of a shotgun round being chambered. That metal "cla-chunk" sound — it's like no other in the world. It's the original all-guy-double-boner-alarm clock.

And it goes off right next to my head.

"You awake?" asks Denver, as he rests a box of 12-gauge shells on my cojones.

Outside, we are one inch into a four inches of rain day. The ¼ mile dirt/stone driveway is now a river of mud. A whitewater driveway.

Denver has been up for an hour. Alone. Just him, his maps, and duct tape. From experience, I know that this is not necessarily a good thing.

"Monkeys like to smell their fingers after picking their butt cracks. That's curiosity; you know what I mean."

180

I don't. I reply, "Uh-huh," and out on the porch and listening through the window, Spinner says, "Fuck yeah."

"I don't believe for a minute that Bigfoot is curious about humans." Another shell is racked into place. One less on the family jewels. "There is no evidence that Bigfoot is attracted to singing, screaming, pounding pans, or normal conversation. No one has proven that. Searching for Bigfoot shouldn't be any different from hunting a wily big game animal. Scout the area...look for food sources...find water...sit still...track the wind. Lock your scent, minimize movement, have Bigfoot come to you. Understand terrain, how it moves on trails. Come here...look at this."

Very gently moving the bullets off the boys, I slide out of bed and follow him into what used to be the cabin dining room. It now looks like a pine-paneled version of NASA.

Under the dining room dead animal horns/antler/and what looks like hoofs chandelier, spread out everywhere, are maps. Maps on the table, maps on the floor, maps duct-taped to the brand-new pine-paneled $500-security-deposit-being-held-by-the-guy-in-Jersey walls.

And Chris sitting there with laminating stuff stuck all over him. MIS meets GPS. "DB...I've got maps of every inch of the terrain around us." All I see are brown and green maps, under almost non-wavy laminate, with a bunch of squiggly-ass lines--some of which are far apart, some of which are very close together.

All this before the first cup of Caffè Verona. I hate camping. Going into the kitchen, I grab my handful of vitamins, swill them down with my morning Coke as I pour Starbucks and look for the fruit I left in the fridge. Finding all the blueberry jelly donuts, I grab just three and plop onto a bar stool next to the granite island.

As I lean over and hit the CD player, the 1988 Eric Clapton Crossroads version of "After Midnight" bounces off the pine, and in spite of himself, Denver tells Chris what a high level super-double-top-secret way for handling fuck-ups on laminate must be. "Don't worry, just take the yellow dry-erase marker, and write over the permanent marker with it, and the permanent marker comes right off. Wipes it clean."

And we wonder why nothing lasts in Washington.

Behind me, Spinner has a pound of bacon frying in three pans. A dozen eggs sits at the ready. He's slicing green peppers with an 8-inch carbon-fiber commando knife.

"I hate them Bigfoot Inc. sissy-men. They don't do planning shit like you do, Den. I've never seen them prepare maps. All they do is take an invading noisy horde of thirty people to some alleged hot spot, where suddenly every sound, or movement is Bigfoot, and everybody gets freaked out thinking they had some encounter. It's just some damn social event."

Spinner is excited, swinging the soufflé bayonet knife to point at Denver's maps. A slice of green pepper flies by my face and lands in Jimmy's lap just as he strikes out Barry Bonds on the big-screen TV connected to his PS2. Happy with his 14th K, he picks up the piece and eats it, not realizing that in his joy of striking out the home-run king, he just popped a vegetable in his mouth.

Chris looks up from a topo map of some swamp, probably trying to GPS his freakin'

wetlands iPod instead of finding Bigfoot trails, and asks, "Bigfoot Inc...hot spots...what?" Chris is a virgin Bigfoot hunter.

Denver, who has been out on several "Bigfoot Expeditions" for research on the Bigfoot book he is writing, walks by Spinner and hands him a peanut butter and jelly sandwich, and all is suddenly calm in Spinner-land. "Chris, when we say Bigfoot Incorporated we don't mean anyone in particular...just all the folks out there making a buck on some theoretical mythic beast and the people who desperately want Bigfoot to be. Bigfoot is a religion to many in the Bigfoot Community…and there's money to be made."

Spinner mumbles something, but the PB & J in his mouth is keeping him safe from a libel suit.

"Hot spots, Chris," Denver says, "are places of suspected Bigfoot activity, and Bigfoot expeditions go to hot spot after hot spot, month after month. Moving about to separate locations for a day or two is simply about money, guy, and not serious Bigfoot research. Once you identify a hotspot, you need to conduct advanced, surreptitious surveillance and reconnaissance for months or years…you're not going to find anything doing drive-bys."

This from a man who has been in hot spots all over the world, facing monsters of the non- theoretical kind.

A FACEFUL OF DIRT

It's a Jack the Ripper lurking behind a rainy mist kind of night.

Pitch black, low-hung ground fog, drizzle that runs down your back. Only a memory of where the stars once were.

N 43° 41′ 48″ W 73° 58′ 05″… another Denver-declared "perfect Bigfoot turnpike."

I like to think of it as an old logging road, preferring as I do to see red-plaid lumberjacks to 10-foot-tall, 1,500-pound hairy monsters, not to mention the bears, cougars, rattlesnakes, and mountain lions that the rangers warned us about. Back in civilization, when I had learned of the deadly-animal-to-human population in the area we were to be hunting, I emailed the following to Denver, cc'd to Spinner:

From: <u>don.barone@gmail.com</u>
To: <u>denverr@aplacewecantevensayexsists</u>
Cc: <u>spinner@prettymuchsameasabove</u>
Subject: Monster Tour 2006
Bring WEAPONS!!!!!!!
Very truly yours, db

Which they did...Denver a sweet, black, long-barreled 12-gauge, and Spinner--who would only admit to a few pistols, "and other things."

On point, with Gen-3 night vision dialed up high, is Jimmy. Behind him, a volleyball teammate from our hometown of Charmington, CT: Matt, who has Jimmy by a week of experience in the woods.

Behind Matt is his father Scott, some sort of bigwig at GE, about whom I specifically told Denver and Spinner, "Please take care of this guy...don't let anything happen. I think he has something to do with our lights."

Denver stalks behind Scott, then comes Chris with Spinner, who is walking backwards in case we missed some sort of Bigfoot off-ramp.

Suddenly, Spinner yells in a voice that even makes crack dealers' buttholes pucker, "GET OFF THE TRAIL. NOW!!!!!"

And all you see are asses and elbows flying off into the brush. Even the guy who quite possibly owns my fridge and dishwasher back home is now rolling through Adirondack underbrush.

Spinner "finds his spot" off to the left, with a clear view of what was barreling down the path. Lots of metal clicks and whirls and things being unsheathed, as he must smell Armageddon downwind.

Denver, in one quick move to the right, becomwa as invisible as a skinny man at an All-U- Can-Eat buffet. That is, until Chris, who up until this exact moment had only dived for cover in Xbox video war-games, starts feeling up Denver's ass.

As Denver will later relate: "I'm laying there on the ground trying to size up the approaching foe, when suddenly I'm getting an ass massage. So I say, 'Who's touching me?' at which point I hear this tiny voice say, 'Chris.'"

"So I yell, 'Get your fingers off my ass...and get down,' at which point he kneels down like a dog on all fours...so I scream, 'Face in the dirt...face in the dirt!'" Which even on the battlefield is sometimes not taken quite literally, something the Xbox war-game programmers never mentioned to Chris, who now has his face firmly planted in genuine Adirondack Park goop.

At pucker-inducing moments like the one we found ourselves in, you become protective of your kin. In fact, the very last thing I said to Denver and Spinner — after warning them of my potential electricity problem with GE should they somehow lose Scott — was exactly this: "Whatever you do, make sure Jimmy is safe. Barb is convinced Bigfoot is going to carry him off somewhere...so watch him."

Both nod; they may be warriors, but they still don't want to mess with Barb. Especially if they're stuck in that awkward position of trying to explain why they let Sasquatch carry off her only son.

Of course, they completely forget their solemn promise when it's each man for his own ass and elbows time. From my day-and-a-half of experience woodsman son, Jim, comes this account of what happened next:

"I'm just standing there in the middle of the trail, looking straight down it, and I hear something...I can't see anything, but whatever it is it's closing fast. Suddenly I realize the noise is an

engine, and from around a bend comes this headlight ...which, since I'm looking at it with Gen-3 night vision, blinds me. So, I take off the night vision, one eye blind now, and I look up, look to the side, look behind me...and I'm the only damn person on the trail."

That is correct. Barb and Don's baby boy was standing up flag-pole straight in the middle of a Bigfoot Turnpike while some sort of motorized Sasquatch heading straight at him. And his protectors, nowhere to be found. Faces in the dirt.

"Then I hear Spinner yelling, 'Get off the trail...GET OFF THE TRAIL! GET DOWN...HIDE!'" And since this is pretty much the first time in Jim's life that he's faced the threat of being run over, and since I, as a father, had pretty much warned him about the dangers of smoking and the evils of weed, while inexplicably forgetting the father/son lecture dealing with the ass-and-elbows method of the tuck-and-roll approach to avoid oncoming vehicles, he was on his own. The boy did the best he could.

Which was moving a little to the side, bending over, and covering his face with his hands.

And closing his eyes.

Let me tell you, a six-foot-something volleyball player does not fold down much into anything remotely invisible. And as a loving, caring person, I'm thinking, just how much could a gas generator be if I should happen to throw the GE bigwig out into the path in a humanitarian attempt to save my son? It's not like I would be losing cable.

And just as I reached for Scott, two knuckleheads on ATV's flew by, and across the trail, stooped over but safe, I could see Jimmy looking at me from between his fingers. A wave of pure fatherly joy engulfed me as I realized my son was not seized by Sasquatch, and that I still would have electric lights.

BACON, A CHICKEN,
AND PEANUT BUTTER SANDWICHES

Bait.

We need bait.

So far, after spending several hours out in the Adirondack woods on two consecutive nights, we have yet to see a freaking animal OF ANY KIND, let alone a theoretical mythic beast.

We did hear a dog bark.

In the spirit of full disclosure, though, I must tell you the alleged bark came right smack dab in the middle of a late-night porch farting contest between Denver and Spinner, and Jimmy swears that if it was indeed a bark, the dog's breath smelled pretty bad.

But in a pristine protected forest filled with streams, marshes, beautiful freshwater lakes, and wild berries growing everywhere, we have somehow managed to pick several areas completely devoid of fauna.

We know there is flora there, because we tucked and rolled through it.

And I tell you this so as to better explain to you, the reader, and to you the guy in Jersey who has my $500-dollar security deposit, why Denver is now walking down the gravel driveway pouring out a bucket of bacon grease behind him.

One man's environmental mishap is another man's bait.

Since we have had no luck going to Bigfoot, we are now hoping to bring Bigfoot to us. With bacon.

And it's working...out of nowhere, a seemingly wild chicken has appeared, and with head cocked, appears to be very interested in Denver. Not exactly a mythic beast, but you have to start somewhere.

Ever since we have arrived at this cabin we have had a creepy feeling that we are not alone here. Normally, since this place needs snow to make money, it's not that often occupied in July...no humans here. So whatever it is out there in the woods got comfortable coming around.

And then we showed up. If beasts have habits, we have just massively fucked up their routine.

That's why, to a man, we feel we are being watched. We've heard what sounds like howls, tree-knocking, and stones banging together — the Bigfoot community trifecta — and once possibly/ maybe/could have been/who knows a rock tossed at the cabin by Bigfoot/unseen neighbor/Spinner trying to scare the hell out of me.

In a spare bedroom, balanced on an open windo sill, we have a 150-watt stereo blasting out a CD that has on it sounds that some folk believe to be Bigfoot talking.

Personally, having now heard this recording played on a loop for almost two days straight, I find the thing to be more than a bit hokey. And since the folks who recorded it never actually saw Bigfoot step up to the mike and start jabbering away, who knows what's making the sounds.

There are howls, which can creep you out, but then there are grunts, shrieks, and jibber- jabber that the Bigfoot community calls "Samurai," which makes sense because to me, it sounds like a bad ninja film soundtrack recorded on a 1970s tape cassette.

And that is what we have blasting out the window, hoping to attract Bigfoot, or more likely, the spirit of Bruce Lee. What bothers me, though, is even if it's a Bigfoot recording, and we don't know that, what we REALLY don't know is what the thing is saying.

With my luck, this alleged Bigfoot is using Bigfootese to say, "The non-hairy creatures are back...run."

Which is why there is bacon grease running down the driveway, our way of editing the CD to say, "But wait! There's bacon."

"You know DB...what we're doing is controversial," says Denver, who, smelling quite similar to a Denny's Grand Slam breakfast, has now joined me on the porch.

Spinner is up on top of a 40-foot rock outcropping behind the cabin and is pegging rocks at the one wild animal we have seen here...the chicken that was following Denver.

"No shit," I say while looking around to make sure my son Jimmy doesn't hear me talk like I warn him not to. "How we going to cook the freaking eggs now without the bacon grease?" A rock lands in what may be the only shallow pool of bacon bits in all of the southern Adirondacks. And the stupid chicken just stands there.

"No, not the bacon grease," says the DOD BLT sitting next to me. "Baiting Bigfoot— using bait to attract Bigfoot—is a controversial subject."

All I can do is turn and look, speechless, at the man who a moment ago was leading a chicken around the yard with bacon grease.

Denver has seen this look before, but by God it never stops him. "Yeah, right now the Bigfoot Inc.s out there are having this debate about if they should even try and bait Bigfoot with food, and I'm serious, DB--some are worried that Bigfoot may have a lactose or gluten intolerance and that bait may make it sick."

I'm thinking, HOW would someone know that? Has someone seen a Bigfoot with hives? Who in their right mind thinks of these things? And should we be baiting Bigfoot with Lactaid instead of lard?

"They're just idiots," yells Spinner as he tries to roll a boulder off the ledge and onto the chicken standing below. "What about that PhD scientist guy we are going to talk to on Tuesday...didn't he say he saw Bigfoot walking his way from the general direction of some fucking restaurant's Dumpster?"

The PhD guy did say that, but not quite in those terms.

So, if bait gives Bigfoot bad poops, we got a problem, because Spinner — not exactly up on the do's and don'ts of the established Bigfoot community — has, until this moment unbeknownst to us, been baiting Bigfoot around the cabin.

From where we sit on the porch, at our 2 o'clock position, 20 yards out are two peanut butter and jelly sandwiches and one grilled cheese.

Even Denver is speechless.

At our 6 o'clock position, 30 yards out and about 7 ½ feet up in a white birch tree, are my son's favorite Little Debbies. And in an area of small bent trees that is supposed to be some sort of Bigfoot street sign, is a paper plate with three Piggly Wiggly Ice Cream Sandwiches on it.

"What are you looking at me like that for?" asks Spinner, which is not a rhetorical question, because we could be looking at him like we are, one, in disbelief about what he has done to our food supplies; or two, because he is now standing on the porch steps with a semi-flat dead chicken in his hand.

RANGER VIC

Both Denver and Spinner have explained this to me twice now, but I'm still clueless.

Even though we have a dining room that has more maps than NATO, we need more.

They're trying to buy a map of a wilderness area where no one's ever been before. And in some miracle of mapmaking, someone has one of those to sell.

And I'm looking at it now, along with the stuffed dead fox on the counter, and under the watchful eye of a stuffed dead owl perched on what is probably a stuffed dead tree limb.

190

Welcome to Ranger Vic's bait, tackle, bullets, and stuffed things shop.

Unfurled in front of me, one corner held in place by a brass .50-caliber bullet, the other corner kept in place by lead fishing weights, is yet another map. It's sort of like all the other ones we have taped up on the cabin's pine walls, all squiggly lines and shit, except for the middle of it where Denver is pointing.

He's pointing to this huge part of the map that has absolutely nothing drawn in. All around it lines are drawn close together, and far apart, little cross things that are supposed to be swamps, creek lines, fatter creek lines that are supposed to be rivers, and then the part of the map, that is just...paper.

And that is what Denver and Spinner want. "We need to go there," Denver says to Ranger Vic while pointing to a spot on the map that has no there there. We are actually going to give this guy $5.99 for a map that will lead us to nowhere.

This is why outdoor type guys scare the crap out of me.

And Ranger Vic has no problem telling them how to get to the one spot on the map that is not mapped. In a conversation for the ages, Ranger Vic points to the blank paper part of the map: "Right about here is a trail you can't really see because it isn't on this map." And Denver nods his head yes as he looks at the unmapped trail that is not there on a blank section of map.

Ranger Vic points inside the blank area. "You can't see it here, but about here's a pond where we found this dead camper once; you follow the trail north around the pond." Ranger Vic's finger is actually tracing around the tip of a pond that is not on the map. "And you come out to this trail that is probably right about here." He could probably be more exact if it were actually mapped.

The finger lifts about two inches off the map and comes down hard enough that the tip turns white. "And this right here is where you want to end up." As best I can tell, Denver and Spinner want to be about a quarter inch left of Ranger Vic's hangnail, a third of an inch south of the cigarette ash that just fell on the map.

"Don't mind me for asking, but why you folks want to go there?" At which point, all the folks there turn and look directly at me. And I do believe that then and there is when Ranger Vic notices me for the first time as I stand in a store that displays camouflage baby bibs, me all ablaze in my bright-red, palm tree and martini glass Tommy Bahama Hawaiian shirt.

"We're looking for Bigfoot."

And I watch his eyes, a hunter's eyes, move from the bikini-clad woman in the martini glass on my left boob, up to my scraggly-ass shoulder-length hair, down to the palm tree on my right boob, then quickly check to see where my hands were, pausing at my Movado watch before finally coming to rest on the bridge of my nose.

At which point I know how a deer must feel.

And this is what the King of all Outdoors says back to me. "Hmmmpf. Well, you know, I've been a ranger for thirty-plus years in these woods, and I know that we have moose here, but I ain't never seen a one."

And we all know at that point that Ranger Vic is one cool dude. In a neighborly way, Ranger Vic has just told us that even if you don't see something, it doesn't mean it's not there...which is how he can read maps that don't have any lines.

So we talk, and he listens, never once judging us as we question him about theoretical mythic beasts. He tells tales of how he and his dog used to walk the trails alone at night, making sure the campers were safe and that hunters weren't shooting things they ought not to be, "making sure everyone followed the rules to keep this place beautiful as can be." As we say goodbye and start to leave, he tells us to be careful and watch out for bears. "You'll hear them out there at night talking to one another."

I, in my Tommy Bahama, think nothing of it...Denver and Spinner, in their camouflage gear, stop dead.

At the same time, Denver says, "Excuse me?" as Spinner says, "What do you mean, talking to one another?"

At which point Denver leans over to me, and resting a hand on the palm tree on my shoulder, says, "DB, I've been in the woods all my life and I've never heard anything about bears talking to one another."

And then, Ranger Vic starts howling, and grunting, and warbling with one final rising octave howl. And I stopped dead.

Because a foot in front of us, with a stuffed dead fox to his right, a stuffed dead owl over his shoulder, homemade fishing flies stuck in his shirt, Ranger Vic has just perfectly mimicked the sound recorded on the "Bigfoot Vocalizations" CD. A CD I am sure he has never heard.

So we play him the CD we have in the truck. Sitting patiently in the passenger seat, Ranger Vic waits as Denver ejects The Wiggles CD and cues up the Bigfoot disc to the part that has the howls.

Ranger Vic listens once, twice, three times, then says, "Yep... them's bears."

A sound of something purportedly recorded on the West Coast is now firmly placed on the East Coast.

"Been hearing them all my life around here."

"Denver, pause it a minute will ya?" I say, as I am about to ask Ranger Vic the money question. "That CD is allegedly a recording of Bigfoot vocalizations; that supposedly is a Bigfoot howl."

Turning from me, Ranger Vic looks over at Denver, and the

glimpse of him I catch in the rear-view mirror tells me that he isn't about to go down that path. He never tells us whether he believed in Bigfoot or not, and I know he never will. "Don't know about that there." Deliberate speech from a man used to dealing with strangers. "But, sounds to me like bear."

Money question number two: "Vic...have you ever seen a bear make that sound?" Short, sweet, to the point, like Ranger Vic. "Can't say that I have."

And then Denver re-hits the pause button...and through six Ford speakers come the alleged Bigfoot Samurai jibber-jabber vocalizations, and within three twirls of the toothpick in Ranger Vic's mouth...we've lost him. Stranger credibility factor of zero. "Well, got to go...wife wants me to fix the roof before winter."

This is July, and it isn't a big roof. But what Ranger Vic did, sitting there in Denver's Ford Expedition, was tell us that whatever those sounds were, they were also echoing through these Adirondack woods.

THE BIGFOOT WHISTLER
AND THE CHAINSMOKING ENGLISHMAN

Deep in the nighttime woods of the Pacific Northwest, Tracy, a twenty-something-year-old college student walks alone, whistling and singing.

She's serenading Bigfoot. And she's hoping he howls back, in tune or not.

We brought her here to the Adirondacks in the hope her songs would bring Bigfoot to us.

You need to know, up front, that Tracy is a true believer in Bigfoot. Because she's seen it. Twice, apparently. But taking a lesson out of Ranger Vic's school of open-mindedness means that just because I haven't seen Tracy's moose/Bigfoot...doesn't mean it isn't there.

Wacky or not, this woman isn't content to search for Bigfoot on Google or in the many Bigfoot internet chat boards. No, she scours the woods alone looking for the creature, and that means she has bigger balls than I do. I respect that.

She also has a chain-smoking Englishman boyfriend named Mark, and she brought him, too. He is not quite such a believer, telling Denver he thinks most Bigfoot expeditions are simply social gatherings. Spinner likes him right away.

Mark and Tracy arrived at the cabin around 2:00 a.m., after flying all day from Seattle. And even though neither one brought hiking boots, clothes, rain gear, or equipment, they wanted to search for Bigfoot tout de suite.

I wanted to go to bed, which I did. So, Denver and Chris took them into the woods. "Within the first ten minutes, Tracy thought she heard a howl," says Denver, who took them back to one of the places where we couldn't find any living animals. "While walking, we talked in normal voices, which she said would help attract Bigfoot." Mark was several yards behind them in his cloud of smoke.

And that's when she started signing and whistling "Twinkle, Twinkle, Little Star" to Sasquatch. Spinner asked her later in the expedition if she took requests. There was no answer.

And it was about this time that Chris saw his first Bigfoot. Denver explains, "It's about 2:30 a.m....I've been up forever...we're moving along railroad tracks with Tracy whistling, Mark hacking up a lung, when suddenly Chris says to me, 'I think there's a Bigfoot over there.' Naturally, I stop.

"Using the Gen-3's, I follow Chris's shaking finger to a small

open meadow beside the tracks...and I find myself looking at what seems to be a bear's ass." He's telling me this at 3:45 a.m., which is why I asked him, "Whose bare ass?" and I raise my head just enough to make sure Spinner is still sound asleep in his bed. He is.

Denver looked over too; it's always good to have two sources when dealing with Spinner. "Turns out, Chris's Bigfoot was just a shadow cast by the moon on some branches of a hardwood tree. We went on for a while but never left the trail, because Tracy says that Bigfoot uses trails too. She also told me that Bigfoot is attracted to psychics, and when I asked her if she was psychic, she said, 'Why do you ask?'"

I'm hoping that Jimmy is asleep and not hearing any of this, because when I get home and Barb asks, "How was the hunt?"' I plan on skipping this part.

"Anything else?" I ask, knowing there probably is.

"Yeah. When we were listening to the Samurai recordings, Tracy said the wailings were actually a Bigfoot saying, 'OOOOOHHHHH MMMMYYYY GGGGOOODDDD' because Bigfoot mimics human voices."

And with that, I put the pillow over my head.

SIGHTINGS

N 43° 48′ 18″ W 73° 46′ 43″

Bigfoot walked here.

And we know that because a PhD Environmental Botanist out doing a wetlands study saw him.

And he took us back to the exact spot. And told us what he witnessed. "It was November 26th, 2003, my fourth day on the site. I was walking out alone at 4:20 p.m., about sunset. I was walking north on a trail back to my car. It was late fall and the leaves were all gone."

We are not going to identify him other than to say he has his doctorate from a Big Ten university, is a well-respected expert in his field, and has studied the forest and its vegetation for the past thirty years.

He was clearly very affected by what he saw. *"I was walking, looking down at my GPS unit, making sure I was on the right trail, and when I looked up, I saw something black walking directly at me.*

"It was coal black, in the woods you don't normally see things that are jet black, except for maybe a bear, but I've seen bears before, and this was not a bear. I stood still just to see just exactly what this was.

"As I stood here looking at it, I realized it was actually moving toward me…this totally dark, human-like figure. My brain was kind of searching for some meaning to it; somehow it impressed my brain as totally strange."

He couldn't see details, but he could make out a head, neck, and shoulders, and thought it was maybe about 6 feet tall.

"The hair on the back of my neck, stood up. I could just feel it all the way up my neck to the top of my head. It was just primal fear, nothing I had ever experienced before. Absolutely gripping fright and flight. There was no desire to stick around. It was get out of here because this was totally strange…it is not within your realm of experience, and it's dangerous."

He then made a decision and came to a realization that I can't imagine making.

"I turned around and made my way relatively carefully, as quietly as possible, to the side trail. At that point, I did stop and remove my camera from my pack, just so that in case it was following

me, I might be able to get a picture of it--so that if it killed me, I would at least have a picture of what killed me."

N 43° 15′ 47″ W 73° 43′ 01″

Bigfoot walked here too: Bob and Michael Dorrer, two local hunters, both saw it, and they brought us back to the trail it walked on.

Bob saw it first: "There was a deer coming down the run. I'm sitting there with a rifle on my lap, and all of a sudden I saw this thing coming down off the mountain."

That was twenty-two years ago, and up until this day, with us, they had never returned to this spot.

Ever.

Bob had the closest, and longest, encounter. "It was all hairy, some kind of creature, probably about five-eight to six feet, and I was looking at it and I was startled. I go, what the hell is that? You know, I'm looking at the thing, I have the rifle on my lap, and I'm looking at the deer. The deer would stop moving every time this thing moved down over the rocks. The agility it had...moving its legs. The arms weren't moving. It was kind of slumped over a little; it kept looking back at the deer. The deer would move a bit, and it would stop, and vice versa.

"It wasn't any more than thirty-five yards in front of me. I was just watching it in awe. What the hell is this thing I'm looking at? It never seen me; the wind was coming down off the mountain, blowing away from me, so it didn't pick up my scent, and I watched the thing for maybe twenty minutes."

He was dressed in camouflage, sitting with his back up to a tree. When it looked at the deer, Bob saw the thing's face. "I could see these coals, eyes. There was no skin — no skin, no flesh, nothing showing. It had reddish-brown long hair. It made no sound at all, moved quietly in the leaves."

Michael, his brother, was on the other side of the mountain when he saw the creature. "There was this bloodcurdling scream, and then as I'm looking down the hill, I see this thing scurry by. I watched it move for thirty to forty seconds, easy."

Two brothers who have been hunting these hills all their lives… leave and don't come back. For twenty-two years.

Michael: "We both got up and left. I have goose bumps right now, talking about it."

Bob: "I think about it every day. It's etched in my mind. I felt shocked. I'm looking at something — what is this thing? Until I got out of the woods and thinking about it…I was thinking, you know, that was a frigging Bigfoot!"

Up until today, in the past twenty-two years, he had only told this story to four people.

After we stopped filming, Bob and Michael took Denver, Spinner, Jimmy, and Chris up the hill to where Michael was sitting when he saw the creature, and to look around, just in case.

As I am talking to Tracy, I am watching the chain-smoking Brit over her shoulder, concerned that if we are indeed in an area known to be frequented by those theoretical mythic beasts, the last thing I want to have happen is some bizarre diplomatic nightmare from having a guest of our country snatched up by Sasquatch. That, and I'm not sure if I can expense the healthcare bills of a chain-smoking Englishman.

That's when I see him flick his cigarette and suddenly bend down to look at the ground. When he looks back up at me, I see on his face that he is considering giving up smoking. Walking over there, I follow the small wisp of tobacco smoke down to the ground, and there, about three inches left of the filter, I ssee what looked like a footprint.

A barefoot footprint. And from a dad used to buying size 12 volleyball shoes, I can tell in an instant it is larger than that. Hitting the talk button on the walkie-talkie, I say, "Denver, Spinner--get your asses back here."

Squawk, squeak, static… "Nice language, Dad," is the reply.

Before Spinner joined a state police squad, he spent years as an evidence tech--the nature of the work, we can't talk about. If anyone would know a footprint, he would. And now he is lying down on the ground with his face about four inches from the dent. "I think I can feel five toes, and there is a clear indentation where a heel would go. We'll never be able to cast it though."

Then he said something that made us all decide to go to lunch. "Looks recent."

THE PREDATOR RV
and
BIGFOOT EXTERMINATORS INC.

It's just Denver and me in the minivan as we head back up the Northway from the Albany airport. Tracy and Mark are winging their way back to their Seattle Sasquatches, leaving the Adirondacks with nothing more than bug bites.

1:20 a.m.…the honest hour: we're both way too tired to lie. I bitch first. "I'm not doing this walk in the woods stuff anymore…I hate freaking nature; it makes me sneeze. This sucks," I say as I put the Sasquatch-searching Sienna on cruise control. Denver is semi-awake now.

"We come here…walk around forever…and all we've seen is a freaking chicken, and we ate that."

"I saw five deer," he says while playing with the hula girl I have stuck on the dash. I know him; he's doing that so he won't have to look at me.

Forgetting that the minivan is on cruise, and not autopilot, I turn completely sideways to talk to him. "Whoopty-doo! I've got three deer eating the freaking roses in my back yard in Charmington right now."

Silence. I hit the satellite radio button, and Cream's "Born under a Bad Sign" comes on.

I take it as a message from God. "Den, there's got to be a better way to do this."

For twenty-eight mile-marker posts, no sound comes from the passenger seat. I know he's either coming up with a plan or is thinking about how he can have me snatched by the government. Finally, he says, "DB, you know that the people we interviewed about Bigfoot had one thing in common?" I can think of a few things, but I let it pass.

"Bigfoot came to them; they weren't tramping around looking for it." This he tells me after we finished six days of doing just that. "We need to make it so Bigfoot comes to us."

"You're forgetting Spinner's peanut butter and jelly and ice cream sandwiches bait." Which reminded me we needed to pick up donuts on the way back.

"But think of this. What if we went where we knew Bigfoot might be--and waited?"

"I'm done with the freakin' woods, you — "In a state-of-the-art RV."

I've got twenty more exits to go; it's going to be a long ride. I dial the cruise up to 80. "Humor me, DB. I've been thinking about this...I bet I could design the greatest attack RV of all time. I'd call it The Predator."

I should have leased the 8-cylinder Sienna. I click cruise up one more notch. At this point you need to know that I am not asking for any details. But they are coming regardless:

"I would take a regular ass Class-A RV [he's talking all those big bus-like things you see heading south around October], make it four-by-four with puncture-resistant tires, wrap-around windshield for the cockpit [you and I call it The Driver's Seat] with NVG [Night Vision Goggle] navigation so it could run lights-out in black mode."

"I would make it so it has a tactical communications suite of VHS, UHF, HF....all designed to look like a luggage rack, and stick a satellite up/down link in the roll-out awning. Maybe even FLIR [forward-looking infrared] cameras and UAV's [unmanned aerial vehicles], including The Dragon Eye and the ever-popular CVG-2002, portable fixed-wing and vertical takeoff and landing unmanned aerial vehicles." *Something, he says, we can park over Bigfoot's ass for hours.*

"I'm on a roll, DB...this could work, this could work." *I'm suspecting it's more of a sugar high.*

"I'd rip out that factory-installed microwave crap and replace it with an after-market mini-forensics/bio lab for DNA, scat, and hair analysis, and toss in a cryogenic platform that will be able to detect a dead Bigfoot in the field."

We'll spend thousands of dollars so we will actually be able to smell the road kill before we run over it. Finally, our exit appears.

"And...and...get this, oh, this is so cool. Should Bigfoot get curious and actually walk up and touch the vehicle, the whole skin of the RV will be touch-sensitive, and nets will fly out and capture the thing. Oh...oh...and I could make some lawn chairs that are really heat-sensing devices and a Weber grill that can detect all the known light and sound frequencies."

The only thing he forgot to add is the AARP sticker on the back. I park my decidedly non-attack Toyota in the cabin driveway, and Denver jumps out and runs into the house to draw up what he wants to take on our next Bigfoot hunt.

Coming inside, I see that Jimmy and Spinner are watching hour 18 of the 24-hour Monster Marathon on the Animal/History/Do Girlee Things to Your House/Creature Channel.

And there, right in front of me, on the big screen TV, is Bigfoot! Our first sighting in the Adirondacks.

It's 2:30 a.m., I forgot the damn donuts, Denver is drawing his Winnebago from hell on what's left of our paper plates, and in fifty inches of high-freakin'-definition plasma TV is the Holy Grail of all things with big feet and bad hair: the Patterson/Gimlin film of an alleged Bigfoot walking by some raggedy ass creek.

I'm thinking, Why in God's name doesn't somebody just shoot the thing?

If I had bought the donuts, I wouldn't be quite this cranky.

"You think that film is real, Dad?" asks Jimmy, who is ready to flip the switch for PS2 so he can beat Spinner for about the eighth time.

I don't know, and I don't care. It's been eight hours since my last glazed jelly log. "Some people say yes, others say there's a zipper on the back. Who knows? I think it's a nice film, but useless. As long as it's in dispute, you can't base squat on it."

"Fuck yeah," was Spinner's technical analysis of the footage.

I go on. "Jim, to me, the only way to solve the Bigfoot is real vs. just a theoretical mythical beast dilemma is by using proven science that can be replicated by any researcher, anywhere. Saying you think the beast is or is not, does this or that, based on that freakin' film, is like watching Mickey Mouse cartoons to study the habits of

203

rodents, for God's sake. You need indisputable evidence, buddy, and it just ain't that."

"DNA is for sissies," says Denver. That coming from a guy designing a high-tech device with crayons on a paper plate. "Bring me the body of the beast, by God." In the loft directly above Denver, I see Chris peeking his head out of the sleeping bag.

"Wake up, MIS boy--I've got a project for you...this is perfect." From years of being around Denver, I know "perfect" is open for interpretation.

Chris, walking down the stairs in his boxers, tee-shirt, and Yankee hat on backwards, gives me this look that says, "Mr. Barone, I know I'm dating your daughter, but do I really have to listen to this man who is now writing something down on a ripped-off Dunkin Donuts box top?"

And I give him the universal middle-aged person's look back that says "Don't blame me, I haven't been in control of anything since the late '80's."

And then, like a Wimbledon Champ, Denver raises the donut lid over his head, and this is what it says: www.bigfootexterminators. com.

And this is what he is shouting: "Take your woods back, America! Your hiking trails, bike paths, lover's lane...HELP PROTECT BAMBI! We are going into the Bigfoot-ridding bidness, boys."

At which point, I go to bed.

CPSIA information can be obtained
at www.ICGtesting.com
Printed in the USA
BVHW040228071220
595076BV00021B/1157